Reading With God

Lectio Divina

David Foster

LONDON • NEW YORK

Continuum

The Tower Building, 11 York Road, London SE1 7NX

15 East 26th Street, New York, NY 10010

www.continuumbooks.com

First published 2005

British Library Cataloguing-in-Publication Data
A catalogue record for this book is available from the British Library.

ISBN: 0-8264-6084-4

Typeset by Aarontype Limited, Easton, Bristol
Printed and bound in Great Britain by MPG Books Ltd, Bodmin, Cornwall

Contents

Foreword

Who wants a life, or to see good days? Think of any crowded place in one of our cities, a shopping mall, a station or airport. People milling around, some more purposeful than others, some in a definite rush – where? We see them, each with their own story to tell, and project to fulfil, but we never ask. Of course not. None of our business. Someone asking opinions we shy away from, nervous of what they want to ask, vexed by the waste of time. Perhaps someone is shaking a tin for donations – another interruption, but small change is no cost, and the badge gives us a slight sense of solidarity in doing good with others around us. What do we really want? Have we ever really thought? No time. But are we ready to make it? Or do we prefer to put the really important questions off? The difficulty with so much of life is that it gives us little help in getting a sense of ourselves as living a life; that is to say, we have careers, holidays, families perhaps, but how easy is it for us to tell our lives as a single story, from beginning to end, with any real sense of a shape to it, with room for all its different elements, a story that says who I am, what I am aiming at, what I am hoping for?

A group of sixth formers once said what they felt the really important questions were, that there was scarcely time to think about. It was a strange list since it was almost timeless, and profoundly religious. They are the questions that lie at the heart of religious faith: who am I? what's the point? what can I hope for? where am I from, and where am I heading? what do I really want, and is it worth it?

This book is about a way we can give ourselves a chance to explore questions like that. It is about how we can learn to tell the story of our lives and, above all, to connect the day-to-day rush and tumble, or just the emptiness, with the big questions of faith. It is written from within the Christian tradition, and it is about how Christians have learnt to tell the story of their faith by learning a way of reading the Bible. The Bible is perhaps the greatest story of faith there is, reaching back through the Old Testament to Abraham and the long history of developing faith in God that shaped not only Jewish religious identity, but also the heart and mind of Jesus and all who have believed in him. This way of reading is called *lectio divina*.

In fact it is far more than a way of reading; it is a way of praying, letting the words of the Bible illuminate our experience and understanding, and using them to nourish a sense of God's presence in our own hearts and minds, so that we can listen to him, and let him help us find ourselves in relation to him. It is an ancient way of reading and praying with the Bible, but its method is one that is nowadays proving more and more valuable in helping people get a deeper and fuller sense of their lives. It has in fact been central to the Christian tradition of prayer, and as a result it has found a place of honour in monastic life generally, and especially among the practices of Benedictine life. But it is not only to monks that God has spoken in the scriptures; and *lectio divina* is not only something monks do.

In the Prologue of his Rule for Monks (verses 14–20), St Benedict imagines God turning up in a crowded marketplace. He describes God looking for workmen to take on, but he does not say what the job is or what he requires. He just asks who wants a life, or to see good days – some recruiting pitch! But God does not actually have any particular job in mind; it is not a question of getting any specific task done. He just asks who wants a life. It is just a question of living well.

The real task, then, is life. St Benedict goes on to outline the monastery as a place where people can get a life like that, and a programme they can follow that will lead them to heaven. But before launching out on that programme, he simply urges those who want to listen to God, to listen to the sweetness of his voice, to find encouragement in the fact that he does not leave us on our own, he is with us and guiding us all the way along the path to life. One of the things that Benedict wants a monastery to be is a place where this word of God can be read and heard, as well as put into practice.

To learn to read the scriptures, to listen to them, to make them the source of a life of prayer and inspiration and guidance for one's daily life, is not only for monks and nuns; it is for all who believe. It is about how to find a way to use the Bible as a way of grounding our lives, whoever we are, and whatever our walk in life. It is about how to listen to God speaking to us as we read the Bible and open our hearts to him.

It is offered to everyone who is seeking God in prayer. For it springs from a belief that prayer is a dialogue with God in which the most important task is to learn to listen to him. We can know a lot about the Bible; but for most of us, we know very little about the word God is speaking to us. *Lectio divina* is a way of learning how to listen to God. Christians believe that God talks to us. This book is written in the belief that the scriptures are a school where we learn to understand God's language – and that they also teach us a language to use in prayer.

There are many books that teach *lectio divina*, but, as with many life-skills, it is easy to get sidetracked into reading lots of books about them rather than using the skills for oneself. The best way is just to get started. This is certainly true when we are trying to develop a taste for reading. The primary purpose of this book is to explore how the scriptures themselves teach us to read them and, in doing so, to open our ears to God. The main focus in what follows will be on the Gospels because that is where Jesus Christ comes through most directly and Jesus is the one who teaches us to listen to God's word. Some texts will be from the letters included in the New Testament; they are a witness to what the first Christian Churches learned from Jesus. We must remember that the Old Testament contains the Jewish scriptures, which were God's word for Jesus, and they have always been read by Jesus' followers. I regret that in a book like this so little can be said about them, but this book is intended only to help people get started.

A word of warning, though. This book is arranged as a series of reflections on short passages of the scriptures that can help us learn to tune in to God's way of speaking to us. The passages are themselves to be used for *lectio divina*. This is not a book to be read quickly. It needs to be used meditatively. The passages can be used in this way even better in conjunction with a Bible where their context and other references can be brought into play. The version used in this book is the Revised Standard Version, but that is not to stop anyone from using another. I have in any case adapted the translation where it seemed awkward. The benefits of comparing versions in *lectio divina* will be considered further on.

This is a handbook; its intention is purely practical. It is no theological study, although I would like to think that, as we learn to listen to God, we may indeed become theologians, in the sense given to the word by the monk Evagrius of Pontus: people who can pray, and speak the words of God to others. At the end of each chapter there are a few more general practical comments. But before we start we must do some ground clearance, and explain more precisely what *lectio divina* is.

Introduction

What is *Lectio Divina*?

Lectio divina is a way of reading. It literally means 'divine reading', which may mean reading 'in a godly kind of way', where we are the readers, or it may say something about the reading we listen to: listening to a 'godly reading'. Or it may involve both meanings. *Lectio divina* is not only about learning to read prayerfully, but to do so with our minds and hearts open to God, as if he were reading his words to us. While we are reading we are always ready to turn to him in prayer as we listen to him.

The title of this book, 'Reading with God', reminds us that *lectio divina* is a way of reading the Bible as part of our relationship with God. I like to think of a triangle linking myself, the scriptures and God: I can read the scriptures to develop a deeper understanding of God; I can find God using the scriptures to help me reach a better understanding of myself; and in my conversation with God, I can begin to get a clearer understanding of how he uses the scriptures to address me and draw me to himself. Always the aim is to deepen my sense of friendship with him and commitment to him.

Lectio divina is an 'active' kind of reading in this sense: we are not just passive listeners to what God has said and done in the past. The words are addressed to us, and we are expected to do something. They are one side of a conversation, to which our prayer and lives are the response. *Lectio divina* is a way of praying, but a prayer where we let God start a conversation, rather than where we are constantly bombarding God with our own agenda and preoccupations. One of the things we are trying to do when we devote ourselves to *lectio divina* is to give God time and space in our minds to be there for us, and for us to give

1

ourselves to him, in adoration and self-offering. It is also a good way to grow in our faith so that we may come to 'have the mind of Christ' (Philippians 2.5) and understand better how to live like him.

In this way, *lectio divina* helps us develop a much deeper sense of our relationship with God, a two-way thing, an awareness of how God is in touch with us at a deep level in our lives, as well as of his presence in the world and in those around us.

A Fourfold Pattern of Prayer

Lectio divina is no more and no less demanding than learning to listen to God speaking to us as we listen to the scriptures. It is a work of prayer to God our Father, through Christ and in the Spirit's power to inspire in us faith, hope and love. It is also worth realizing that it is not something we do on our own with God, a private conversation between him and us. The Church has received the scriptures as the word of God, and our listening to them as such must take place within the life of the Church. That does not mean we cannot read them on our own, but we always listen to them within the communion of faith, hope and committed service of the Church.

In some ways the Church's liturgy teaches us some of the best lessons in how to start. In the Eucharist, for example, in the Liturgy of the Word, we listen to the readings of the Old and New Testaments; there should be silence to allow the word of God to speak in our own hearts through what we hear; our response is shaped by the songs and chants which are themselves drawn from the Spirit-filled texts of the psalms and canticles of scripture. The readings of the Old and New Testaments are chosen to prepare us to listen to Christ himself in the Gospel, the meaning of which for the actual community is then reflected on and explained by the priest in the homily or sermon. The whole Liturgy of the Word is completed by the affirmation of the Church's faith in the Creed (intended as a song of praise) as well as in the Prayer of the Faithful which introduces the worship of God in the Liturgy of the

Eucharist, with its offering of ourselves to him in union with Christ in the Eucharist (thanksgiving) and his feeding us in Communion.

Similarly in the daily prayer of the Church, the Liturgy of the Hours, listening to the word of God forms the central moment of the time of prayer; the reading may indeed be very short, and its pithiness aimed particularly to highlight the particular significance of that time of prayer for the community, but what matters is the way the word is received, the heartfelt response of prayer it invites. So the first, and normally longer, part of the office, after the opening hymn that gathers the community together, consists in the singing of psalms, which is aimed at 'softening up' the community to hear the word of God at a personal level; and, after another short time of silent meditation, the community shares its response in the responsory and canticles that follow before the formal prayers concluding the time of worship.

Among the monks and nuns of the early Church a great deal of time was devoted each day to the scriptures and to prayer, and not only during the frequent times of common prayer that punctuated each day and consecrated it to God. By the Middle Ages, at a time when people had a high regard for putting things into ordered patterns and systems, *lectio divina* was 'sorted' into a tidy scheme as well. The most famous of these was the *Ladder of Monks* by Guigo II, Prior of the Grande Chartreuse, around 1180. As with all patterns, there is a danger of over-schematization and reducing human activity to techniques and performance. But a scheme is a good pedagogic tool and we can learn from it.

The traditional pattern to *lectio divina* had four stages: *lectio – meditatio – oratio – contemplatio*. The pattern implied a process by which the person took the words of scripture from his ears or eyes into his mind (reading or *lectio*), repeated them to himself and chewed them over (*meditatio*), and as they began to be digested, he responded to them in prayer (*oratio*), which initiated a movement of prayer beyond the words to God himself who had spoken with these words, a freer spontaneous moment of adoration (*contemplatio*). With time, words like meditation and contemplation developed highly specialized senses of their own that make them rather misleading terms. But the parallels between this fourfold pattern and the liturgical context out of which it grew are, I hope, clear enough.

The next four chapters reflect this pattern, but somewhat more loosely. They will explore the themes of hearing God's word, receiving it, praying with it, and wondering. In the early times reading was not a silent, mental activity; people tended to read aloud even to themselves. In fact this is not a bad way to do *lectio*, just as it is not a bad way to read poetry or anything that requires a more complex response than is normally expected to what we read. We can scan a newspaper, but we would be fools to read Shakespeare in the same way. Reading aloud teaches us to listen. This is the important element.

To listen we have to open ourselves to someone else and let the speaker set the tone and the agenda. Listening puts us in a relationship with the speaker, and learning to listen to the scripture, rather than just to read it, is the best way to learn that God is talking through the human authors of the Bible. That makes a big difference to how we receive the word. It means learning to tune in to a different level of meaning. Since God is with us and his word is addressed to us, it means that we can respond to what we hear, not only as a piece of literature with our understanding but as a meeting point with God in prayer. Gradually, as we begin to understand a personal meaning in what we receive as God's word, we learn to turn our attention more to the speaker than to what he says. Here prayer expands to a simpler act of adoration of God.

These chapters form the core of this book, but two more have been added to give more space to reflecting on the way *lectio divina* fits into our daily lives and commitments. *Lectio divina* is a word of life, and a life we are invited to share with others. The word of God leads us not only to prayer but also to living by the word. Furthermore, *lectio divina* is a way of shaping our whole lives after the mind of God, and of growing ourselves day by day to a fuller maturity of faith, a fullness of life we will enjoy together with the whole creation when God makes all things new. That is looking towards the horizon; but first we must get down to basics!

Some Basic Presuppositions

Lectio divina is based on some very simple assumptions. They are also profound.

The most important is to believe that scripture is the word of God. This is absolutely fundamental – not only that the scriptures have been inspired by God, but also that they express for us, when we read them in faith, God's personal word of salvation. Only when we listen to the scriptures in faith, hope and love can we expect to hear God addressing us.

The word of God

2 Timothy 3.16–17
[16]All scripture is inspired by God and profitable for teaching, for reproof, for correction, and for training in righteousness, [17]that those who belong to God may be complete, equipped for every good work.

The Bible is more than human words; it is not just a witness to a spiritual tradition, a matter of earthly wisdom. It is God's message and it is directed to us. On the other hand, the word of God is expressed in human language; the books of the Bible reflect in many different ways a history of trying to understand God and articulate his word to mankind. So understanding scripture as God's word must always respect the fact that it is mediated within a collection of human writing as well, and must take into account the kind of writing it is, whether historical, poetic, prophetic and so on. The way it is expressed, the cultural and intellectual history behind the Bible, offers plenty of scope

for theological study, but at the end of the day *lectio divina* is trying to tune in to a divine wavelength and to listen to these texts as God's way of talking to us.

Because God is the author of scripture in this sense, it is possible to use all of scripture in a complementary way to understand the specific meaning for us of a passage. For the whole scripture teaches us to see the world as God's, created and called into judgement by him. But above all, a Christian reading of scripture will see Jesus Christ and his redemption of the world as the key to the meaning of everything.

The scriptures are not just there to be quarried for 'proof texts' in preaching or conversation: it is a literature intended for our 'sanctification', to help us grow in the maturity of Christian holiness, to help us become men and women of God.

Jesus is the key to the meaning of the scriptures, as of all existence

Not only are the scriptures inspired, God speaks in them. Moreover, he speaks through his Son. Here, the Letter to the Hebrews draws a parallel between the word God speaks in the scriptures and the word with which he creates all things.

Hebrews 1.1–2

[1]In many and various ways God spoke of old to our fathers by the prophets; [2]but in these last days he has spoken to us by a Son, whom he appointed the heir of all things, through whom also he created the world. He reflects the glory of God and bears the very stamp of his nature, upholding the universe by his word of power.

From the beginning Christians have seen the Jewish scriptures as pointing to Jesus Christ, who is the fulfilment of the Law and the

Prophets. And certainly the various writings of the New Testament centre on his life, above all his redemption of the world by his death and resurrection, and on the impact of his life in the foundation of the Christian communities of the Acts and letters. So the Gospel of Jesus gives the basic rule of interpretation for our reading of the scriptures. We read them in order to know him and live more faithfully according to his word.

This passage from the Letter to the Hebrews goes even further. The world itself was created by him: the Word by whom God made all things is the word that speaks to us in the Bible. So Jesus helps us to understand the world around us more clearly as a world where God is constantly reaching out to us. We read the scriptures in order to understand the meaning of life.

A word of power in the Holy Spirit

This word of God is alive because of the power of the Holy Spirit. The earliest writings in the New Testament give a vivid sense of the dynamic of God's word in the life of the Christian community. The following two passages need to be read together.

1 Thessalonians 1.4–6

[4]For we know, brothers and sisters, beloved by God, that he has chosen you; [5]for our gospel came to you not only in word, but also in power and in the Holy Spirit and with full conviction. You know what kind of people we proved to be among you for your sake. [6]And you became imitators of us and of the Lord, for you received the word in much affliction, with joy inspired by the Holy Spirit.

1 Thessalonians 2.13

[13]And we also thank God constantly for this, that when you received the word of God which you heard from us, you accepted it not as the word of a human being but as what it really is, the word of God, which is at work in you believers.

Paul's preaching was at a human level, but the effect of that preaching was at a deeper level. At the level of faith, God had opened the ears of their hearts to his word. Paul was only a human instrument bringing the Thessalonians into a new relationship with God, through the power of the Holy Spirit. At that spiritual level they are not only imitators of Paul, but of Jesus Christ in whom they believe, thanks to Paul's preaching. And the word of God they have received is a living word that continues to work in their hearts.

When we read the scriptures in faith, it is the same for us. God's Spirit opens our hearts to listen at a deeper level than merely to human words. The Holy Spirit inspires the scriptures and fills them with meaning for all who listen to them. The same Holy Spirit also dwells in our hearts and helps us tune in to the spiritual meaning of the scriptures. To listen to them like this is to hear God our Father addressing us in love.

The scriptures bring us into a living relationship with God. This is the very simple belief on which the whole of *lectio divina* is founded. For God is not an impersonal cosmic force. He is active, all-powerful and creative. This creative power has a single purpose, ultimately to establish a vital and lasting personal relationship with each of us. We know the question: who made us? God made us. Why did he make us? He made us to know him, to love him, to serve him and to be happy with him forever. His word in the scriptures is his pledge of that faithfulness to us.

A word personally addressed to each of Jesus' disciples

The last two passages really refer to the reception of the gospel by a whole Christian community. They remind us that *lectio divina* is a reading of the scriptures that we do within the faith of the Church.

On the other hand God addresses his word personally to all who would believe. It is something for each of us to take to heart. If we do so, Jesus tells us we will enter into a new relationship with him, and a relationship that we will share with him with his Father.

John 14.23–26

[23]Jesus answered him, 'If someone loves me, they will keep my word, and my Father will love them, and we will come to them and make our home with them. [24]Those who do not love me do not keep my words; and the word which you hear is not mine but the Father's who sent me. [25]These things I have spoken to you, while I am still with you. [26]But the Counsellor, the Holy Spirit, whom the Father will send in my name, he will teach you all things, and bring to your remembrance all that I have said to you.'

Jesus invites us to listen to the scriptures as his word to us. If we tune in to them obediently we will hear them as his word, and also as the word God speaks to us as the Father. This kind of listening is something that the Holy Spirit makes possible. The Holy Spirit remains with us and is the God-given power to learn what God's meaning in these words is for us; he is in our hearts helping us to understand and to 'remember', to connect our reading at one time with our reading at other times, and the reading of the Church as a whole; to connect our lives with the scriptures helps us to connect our lives with the lives of all the faithful.

Jesus speaks here of his coming to us and remaining with us; God makes his home with us. We are his hosts. But his word is a home for us, where he makes us welcome, and where we can find a dwelling place. Elsewhere in the Gospel (John 8.31), it says 'if you continue in my word'; the Greek verb could mean 'stay' or 'dwell', the meaning which is given to it in the Jerusalem Bible translation: 'if you make my word your home'. We will return to

these passages in the final chapter. Here we only need to remark the intimacy that scripture offers us: God dwells with us and we dwell with him.

Fellowship in the Word

The scriptures bring us into a living relationship with God. It is not only a one-to-one relationship, but more truly a fellowship comprising all who gather round Jesus and listen to his word. Jesus speaks of those who listen to the word of God and put it into practice as his family.

Mark 3.31–35

[31]And his mother and his brothers came; and standing outside they sent to him and called him. [32]And a crowd was sitting about him; and they said to him, 'Your mother and your brothers are outside, asking for you.' [33]And he replied, 'Who are my mother and my brothers?' [34]And looking around on those who sat about him, he said, 'Here are my mother and my brothers! [35]Whoever does the will of God is my brother, and sister, and mother.'

The situation here is remarkable. Jesus' mother and family are convinced Jesus is out of his mind and have come to the house where Jesus is teaching in order to take charge of him. Jesus seems to brush them off with this remark about whom he sees as the members of his family. In St Luke's account, where the reason for the visit of his natural family is omitted (Luke 8.21), Jesus puts the brush-off rather differently: 'My mother and my brothers are those who hear the word of God and do it.' Luke witnesses to the central place of scripture in the life of Jesus' family, the Church: it is a privileged place where we may learn God's will. But Luke is precise. It is not just a question of listening to Bible readings, or reading it for ourselves; we have to hear the word of God speaking to us,

and put it into practice. That is how we become members of God's family. *Lectio divina* **tries to provide the best circumstances to do that.**

This fellowship is shared with all who have believed in Christ; it is a fellowship that stretches across time and place, and a fellowship we share with the Father and the Son.

1 John 1.1–4

[1]That which was from the beginning, which we have heard, which we have seen with our eyes, which we have looked upon and touched with our hands, concerning the word of life – [2]the life was made manifest, and we saw it, and testify to it, and proclaim to you the eternal life which was with the Father and was made manifest to us – [3]that which we have seen and heard we proclaim also to you, so that you may have fellowship with us; and our fellowship is with the Father and with his Son Jesus Christ. [4]And we are writing this that our joy may be complete.

The testimony of the scriptures, together with the sacramental celebration of what they testify to, is as close as we ever come to Jesus in this life. But this passage speaks of it as a real contact with him, which is assured through our fellowship with those who have passed the faith on to us. So the Christian community is united through time with all who have known the Lord. This fellowship is expressed in the Liturgy of the Church, but it is grounded on our receiving the word of God in faith.

2 John 9

[9]Anyone who goes ahead and does not abide in the doctrine of Christ does not have God; he who abides in the doctrine has both the Father and the Son.

This very short letter summarizes the commandment of Christ to the single precept that we 'follow love' (v. 6). This is the doctrine of Christ. It is the criterion for fellowship in the Christian community. The language in the letter may be obscure, but it speaks as simply as anywhere else that fellowship grounded on love is a fellowship with God.

A Trinitarian dynamic

Lectio divina therefore engages us with the Church and with Jesus Christ. In him we are caught up in the dynamic of the Trinity itself. The most eloquent example of this insight is the hymn at the start of Paul's letter to the Ephesians (1.3–23), which casts our lives in the grand perspective of God's eternal plan realized for us in Christ.

Ephesians 1.13–18

[13]In him you also, who have heard the word of truth, the gospel of your salvation, and have believed in him, were sealed with the promised Holy Spirit, [14]which is the guarantee of our inheritance until we acquire possession of it, to the praise of his glory. [15]For this reason, because I have heard of your faith in the Lord Jesus and your love toward all the saints, [16]I do not cease to give thanks for you, remembering you in my prayers, [17]that the God of our Lord Jesus Christ, the Father of glory, may give you a spirit of wisdom and of revelation in the knowledge of him, [18]having the eyes of your hearts enlightened, that you may know what is the hope to which he has called you.

This is not the place to give the exegesis of the whole of the hymn, which starts by setting the horizon 'before the foundation of the world' and looks on to the fullness of time. Jesus is the centrepiece, and our redemption and glorification with and in him; everything is to be understood not only in relation to him but, more truly, 'in him' pure and simple – as if to say we cannot understand until we are 'in him'. Paul goes on to remark on his own part in bringing the Ephesians to faith in Christ, a faith that has been passed on to them (and to us) through the word of truth they heard as preaching and which we receive as the scriptures.

But Paul comments here that it is not just a matter of listening to the word of truth; we need the Spirit to guide us and to enlighten our minds and encourage us with hope. This is a living relationship with God that helps us to deepen our reading and understanding, as well as to grow in union with him.

How to get Started

The bulk of this book is about the lessons the Bible teaches about listening to God. But, since it is trying to be practical, this section is intended to say something about how to do *lectio divina*. The simplest way of putting it is to read a passage of scripture slowly and prayerfully; let it become part of you, not just sinking into the mind but, more importantly, taking it into your heart; let it resonate there, listen to any echoes; try to listen (rather than think) to how it seems to apply to you, and let it become the starting point of a prayerful conversation with God, at as personal a level as it seems to invite.

To put it at a little greater length, the following are some practical suggestions for getting started that are the fruit of experience. More will be said at the end of other chapters.

First, we need to clear the deck. Find a good time and a place where you can read prayerfully, but in a fairly relaxed kind of way. The morning is often the best time for *lectio*, before the mind is cluttered with the immediate demands of a day. But an evening time, if they are not too tired, is a time when many find they are more relaxed. In either case, the way we read will reflect the time, looking ahead or reflecting on the day past. We do not need a long time for *lectio*, but, as with a conversation with a friend whom one has not seen for a while, it is obviously better if we can expect not to be disturbed or preoccupied by other things.

Second, we need to begin *lectio* in a context of prayer. Put yourself in the presence of God. Let go of the immediate things on your mind, and turn your heart to God who dwells within. Think of the Father who creates you and all things by his word; of the Son who calls us to be not only his disciples, but also his brothers and sisters, who is the Way, the Truth and the Life; and of the Holy Spirit who searches all things, even the depths of God, who inspires the scriptures with the word of God which heals us and guides us. Pray that the Spirit will help you hear and learn from the word that God speaks in our hearts, and that you may feed on that word by faith and with thanksgiving.

Third, we can start our reading. It is hard to suggest what passages of scripture to begin with, it depends so much on the individual. On the whole there is a lot to be said for beginning with a Gospel, where we can really get to know Jesus. Mark or Luke might be easier than Matthew or John, where the gospel story is presented in a more overt theological frame of reference. On the other hand, the letters which follow the Gospels and Acts give their own introduction to a deeper understanding of Christ as well as of the dynamic of a Christian life, and these may suit someone who is already familiar with the Gospels at a certain level of understanding. It is a hardy soul who would begin the practice of *lectio divina* with the first chapter of Genesis, and work valiantly through to the end of the Apocalypse! Apart from anything else, an understanding of Jesus and of the New Testament is a great help in approaching the Old Testament in a Christian way.

There are many other ways into the scriptures from which to choose. It is important to read a book as a whole, or as good as whole. Avoid being too selective, and never just 'dip in'. A number of Bible reading programmes are available which can provide a structured course of reading the scriptures. These can be a good basis for getting started, so long as we remember *lectio divina* is a different thing from Bible study.

We still have to learn to listen to what God may be saying to us and to make our own response to that in prayer. Those who are regular churchgoers may prefer to follow the cycles of reading that are used in church on Sunday, or during the week. The difficulty is the way these cycles have to chop and change to fit the liturgical year. They are excellent for the way they allow us to listen to a whole Gospel, although the other readings have to be very selective, and not always helpfully so. But they have the merit of consistency and of allowing the Church's annual celebration of the mystery of Christ to give shape to one's own life of prayer. I have to say that this is the approach I prefer myself for the Gospels, and which I would recommend to someone starting. For other books, I would take one that is being read at the time in the Lectionary, take my time and read it more completely in my own Bible. The only thing is to find a way that works for you, and to stick to it in order to get to know the scriptures and how to work with them.

Fourth, how to read. This is what we have to take trouble to learn. In general, read a shortish passage slowly and prayerfully. A missal or lectionary, which has the readings laid out for use in Church, will have done the breaking up for you. But if you are working with the Bible itself, take a book of the Bible bit by bit – the section divisions (and the subtitles) in some modern Bibles are useful. Probably you should read for not more than five minutes or so. If there is a bigger section, try reading the whole of it through in order to get the general shape, but go back and start again; and be ready to slow down even more, to take things a sentence at a time, and even word by word, mulling things over, and not being afraid to let your reading prompt the mind to wander a bit.

To get a clearer sense of reading as listening, it is often good to read aloud and listen to the words with your ears rather than your mind. This is what the ancients did, and it is what we all do in Church when we listen to the word of God. That is how some people have to learn to listen to the words in the head. We should learn to listen so that we can 'read, mark, learn and inwardly digest' the scriptures, as Cranmer wrote in his prayer for the second Sunday of Advent. Speed-reading is the absolute enemy of *lectio divina*.

Fifth, we need to let reading turn into meditation and prayer. Listen carefully to the way the passage, a phrase or a word seems to speak to you and to resonate with your experience. Pay attention to that, and consider what makes it prominent. That is the point at which to listen out for something God may guide you to reflect on in prayer, either about himself or about you and your life. Something may strike at once, in which case you just need to receive it gently and in prayer listen to it more quietly. Sometimes the resonance or echo is less obvious, but try listening to the echo and reflect prayerfully how God may be suggesting something. The idea is to let the reading guide one's thoughts and attitudes to things, which it will do by the way we are able to create connections between what we read and everything else. This is where the conversation with God can sometimes begin. But always turn your thoughts towards God and share them with him.

A passage may make little or no impression, but that does not matter. Share the passage with the Lord; he may invite you to consider something in relation to it; he may prefer you to carry on with the reading. Above all do not hurry. Let God take as much time as he needs to speak. Just keep the heart quiet enough to listen.

If we are reading prayerfully, listening to God, we may find that we begin to pray rather than to read. It may be hard to tell the difference between our prayerful reading and our prayerful response to our (or rather, God's) reading. That does not matter. Neither does it matter if our prayer seems hardly to form itself into words or clear ideas: the Spirit searches the heart and we do not know how to pray as we ought . . . Just remember that God is close to us and between close friends a great deal can be left unsaid.

Finally, how to come to an end. At the end of the time we can pray with thanksgiving, and make more specific prayers for people or needs of our own that have come into our time of *lectio*, and especially that we may live the rest of the day in the light of God's word. A good practice to develop is to choose a 'word', a short phrase or sentence which has been important in our *lectio*, either in what we have read or another 'word' prompted by our reading, which we can take with us as a companion for the day. Keep a note of it and return to it in the course of the day. Let it be a word of life, food for the journey. It can be a focus for a time of prayer later in the day.

Chapter One:
Hearing the Word

The first thing in *lectio divina* is to hear the word of God. God speaks to us in all sorts of ways, in the circumstances of our life and through the people we live with. But the place where we really learn to listen to God is when we listen to his word in the scriptures. This is the best school for learning how to tune in to him in other contexts.

The first part of *lectio divina* is traditionally called 'reading'. It is in the time and space that we make for reading the scriptures for ourselves that we generally have the best opportunity to listen and respond to the word of God prayerfully. But it is a little misleading. There are all sorts of ways of reading and something has already been said about the special character of 'divine' or 'godly' reading. In this chapter something more will be said about reading in the practical section at the end. The main thing in our reading is to learn to listen. In a strange way, I think, to listen is more important than to understand. There are plenty of places where the disciples simply failed to understand, but that did not stop them listening to Jesus, nor did it stop Jesus teaching them. But clearly, the important thing is to listen to the scriptures as part of a conversation with Jesus.

Listening to the scriptures is not as easy as it may seem. We may know how to read a text like the Bible, and have some good understanding of its literary quality, historical context and theological meaning, but listening to the Bible is something different. Especially when what we need to learn is to tune in to God speaking to us. The best way is, I think, to try to listen to Jesus reading the scriptures to you. If we believe that Jesus is the Word of God, if we want to tune in to God speaking in the scriptures, we need to tune in to Jesus, who is that Word. To listen to God is to pick out the voice of Jesus echoing through the Bible in our own hearts. So a good way to practise the initial reading of a passage is to put yourself in God's presence with Jesus there to read the scripture to you. You can find a bit more on this at the end of the chapter.

Historically, in fact, the scriptures were designed to be listened to. Even though both Jews and Christians valued literacy precisely because of the place of sacred scripture in the life of their communities, the natural setting for reading them was in liturgical gatherings, in synagogues and churches. In the description of the reading of the Law after the return from the Babylonian exile (Nehemiah 8.1–18) we have an early example of the method in practice; the scripture is read, translated so that people could make sense of the words until they were understood; the people were attentive and responded with their hearts, weeping and with worship. Christians most naturally listened to God's word as it was being proclaimed in the public celebration of the Liturgy of the Word at the Eucharist and, for monks, in the meditative listening to the scriptures as they were read in the community Liturgy of the Hours, especially during Vigils, or the Night Office.

This liturgical setting for the reading (or singing) of the scriptures still has much to teach us as we practise *lectio divina* for ourselves. Just as it is the central element in the common prayer of the faithful, so it can be for our personal prayer. First, *lectio* starts not by our doing something to a text we have taken into our hands; so often reading has a specific purpose of our own in view, whether it be flicking through a timetable, reading a business report or unwinding with a 'good read' on holiday. When we focus on listening rather than on reading, it is what we hear, not our own needs and objectives, that should be the point of the activity: someone else's agenda. And someone else's pace too. That is the second lesson we learn. Listening, we have to take it as it comes; someone else is in charge of the words. Third, but not least important, is the fact that listening to scripture in the Church's liturgy we learn to approach it in the kind of

19

way which helps us tune in to God's word, rather than the human medium of words, printing and so on.

When we read the scriptures for ourselves as *lectio divina*, then, we have to take a bit of a back seat. But putting ourselves into a pew should not mean we have to make ourselves uncomfortable! It is just that we should put ourselves at the service of the scriptures, not put the scriptures at ours.

Something has already been said in the introduction about how to set about the practicalities of reading in *lectio divina*. We really only need to remember that within the process of our reading God is speaking his word to us; our job is simply to tune in to that and receive it in the right kind of way. So this is the place to say something more about listening. It is not something that comes easily to everyone but, as with all natural abilities, we get better by working at it, and *lectio divina* also helps us become better listeners. In the ordinary way of things, listening takes time; it means giving time to another person. Moreover, we need to take some time first to quieten down ourselves. Ideally, that means clearing our minds, or letting our minds clear, of whatever clutters our mental and emotional space; that gives us space in which to receive what God wants to say. If we can only become more clearly aware of the different kinds of noise in our own minds, it will be easier to avoid it interfering with what another person may want to say to us, even God.

Self-awareness (as opposed to self-absorption) is really the key to awareness of anyone else, and understanding what they are trying to say will not always be simply a matter of the meaning of the words the other person utters. We have to learn to pick up other signals. It is similar if we want to hear God's word. Patience is needed, so that we can begin to let God introduce himself to us through the scriptures. This is especially so, as we need to get used to the way God uses human language and literary forms to address us. These are not instantly accessible or familiar to us. There is a section about this at the end of the chapter.

In the passages that follow we shall first of all consider some cases of people listening to Jesus; what it was like for them to hear him may give some interesting clues about what to expect ourselves.

Hearing Jesus

There is a story at the start of Jesus' public ministry where he is in fact reading the scriptures to people. All the Synoptic Gospels suggest that Jesus started his work teaching in synagogues and healing the sick. *Lectio divina* does not need to be done in church, and it is usually done on our own; but this passage gives a very good introduction to the way we should learn to listen.

Luke 4.16–22

[16]And he came to Nazareth, where he had been brought up; and he went to the synagogue, as his custom was, on the Sabbath day. And he stood up to read; [17]and there was given to him the book of the prophet Isaiah. He opened the book and found the place where it was written, [18]'The Spirit of the Lord is upon me, because he has anointed me to preach good news to the poor. He has sent me to proclaim release to the captives and recovering of sight to the blind, to set at liberty those who are oppressed, [19]to proclaim the acceptable year of the Lord.' [20]And he closed the book, and gave it back to the attendant, and sat down; and the eyes of all in the synagogue were fixed on him. [21]And he began to say to them, 'Today this scripture has been fulfilled in your hearing.' [22]And all spoke well of him, and wondered at the gracious words that proceeded out of his mouth.

Perhaps the first step in learning to listen to the scriptures as the word of God is to think of ourselves, as it were, in the synagogue in Nazareth, listening to Jesus read them to us. The second thing is for us to try to listen to what Jesus may be trying to say to us

with them. The first step is often enough for us to avoid reading being just reading; we are already letting the scriptures be a medium of communication. And it is probably easiest to find a personal resonance in what we hear once we let the words be spoken to us by Jesus.

The last part of the story offers some further hints. We must let Jesus take his time, to sit down and begin to teach. It is better to focus our attention on him perhaps more than on the reading: we let him unfold the meaning. We will discover the meaning relevant for *lectio divina* not in the past, but in the present. The passage Jesus read in Nazareth (Isaiah 61) is one of many in the Jewish scriptures that look directly ahead to Jesus himself, and we understand it in a special way when we see it fulfilled in Jesus. But we could also hear the 'today in your hearing' to refer to ourselves; Jesus is now at work in our hearts exploring the scriptures for us, so that we can hear the good news and find freedom and new vision. Those are the themes, at any rate, that we should try to tune into as we listen to the scriptures.

Finally, the last sentence gives a useful hint about how to begin finding a focal point in what we read for the next movement in *lectio*, the move to meditation. As we read, rather slowly and prayerfully, letting Jesus read the passage to us, being ready to stop and think about things as we go along, but not so that we get bogged down in details, the chances are we will find that words, phrases, ideas catch our attention by their graciousness. That is what we should be on the lookout for. There is much that is hard to read in the scriptures, especially at the outset; but they have a beauty to them, strange at first, sometimes, but the beauty with which they stir our hearts is the point at which we can normally begin to tune in to their divine meaning. The subject matter of what we read may not be beautiful in itself: the crucifixion of Jesus, for instance, is horrifying. But it is told

22

beautifully. And therein lies the faith of the human writer and the power of God to work with human language to draw us in faith to himself.

Teaching with Authority

Other passages in the Gospels home in on the way Jesus talks. This is the passage in Mark parallel to the above.

Mark 1.21–28

[21]And they went into Capernaum; and immediately on the Sabbath he entered the synagogue and taught. [22]And they were astonished at his teaching, for he taught them as one who had authority, and not as the scribes. [23]And immediately there was in their synagogue a man with an unclean spirit; [24]and he cried out, 'What have you to do with us, Jesus of Nazareth? Have you come to destroy us? I know who you are, the Holy One of God.' [25]But Jesus rebuked him, saying, 'Be silent, and come out of him!' [26]And the unclean spirit, convulsing him and crying with a loud voice, came out of him. [27]And they were all amazed, so that they questioned among themselves, saying, 'What is this? A new teaching! With authority he commands even the unclean spirits, and they obey him.' [28]And at once his fame spread everywhere throughout all the surrounding region of Galilee.

This passage gives a testimony to the characteristic style of Jesus' teaching similar to Luke's. However, here the power of Jesus is recognized by evil spirits and people witness to Jesus' authority over them. But the same power Jesus shows over the evil spirits can be exercised in our hearts too. Jesus never steps in against our will; but if we ask him, he can turn our hardness of heart, our deafness or coldness – whatever stands in his way – to an attitude of loving attentiveness, a fertile receptiveness to his word, an attitude that can wonder at the beauty of what he says.

To take up a metaphor from elsewhere in the Gospels, we need to let the word of God act as yeast does to leaven the dough of our lives and make it into fresh bread. But this passage gives us a warning not to jump too quickly to the conclusion that this is easy. The word of God will be resisted by what is recalcitrant to it. So the passage gives another hint towards learning how to hear the word of God; we not only listen out for what is beautiful and gracious in what we hear, but we also have to be ready to find some of it challenging, and to pray for the self-knowledge that may be inviting us to explore. This is another way into meditation.

Jesus the Lawgiver

Jesus' speaking with a unique tone of voice is found elsewhere in the Gospels. In Matthew the comment is made at the end of the Sermon on the Mount. The Gospels show us Jesus teaching not only in the synagogue, but also on the mountain, on the plain, on the shores by the lake, on the road, as well as in people's houses. It certainly looks as though he did not find the synagogue the easiest place to reach out to people. There is a lesson for us in that. Often Jesus can speak most directly to us in very ordinary circumstances of our life, if we are able to hear his voice trying to catch our attention. One thing we can try to do in our *lectio divina*, then, is to try to catch the tone in the way God speaks his word, perhaps better, try to find the wavelength in our hearts where we can tune in to him. But, in general, I think we will learn to do this more easily by connecting the way we listen to his words to the ordinary contexts and relationships of our lives. We must not think Jesus only speaks to us, as it were, in church or when we are wearing our Sunday best!

Matthew has Jesus open his great sermon on the mountain (chs 5–7) no doubt, as commentaries will point out, in order to present Jesus as the new Moses, the giver of the new law to God's people.

Matthew 5.1–2; 7.28–29

[1]Seeing the crowds, he went up on the mountain, and when he sat down his disciples came to him. [2]And he opened his mouth and taught them . . .

[28]And when Jesus finished these sayings, the crowds were astonished at his teaching, [29]for he taught them as one who had authority, and not as their scribes.

Someone who is well enough versed in the Old Testament background to passages like this will be able to pick out and reflect on the way Jesus fulfils the promises God made to Israel, rather as he tries to do himself in the synagogue at Capernaum. A more personal *lectio* may simply dwell on the fact that Jesus goes up the mountain because he sees us, and he wants to be seen and heard. And he takes the trouble to sit down with those who wish to listen to him. But do we go to him to do so? How do we come to him? How ready are we to listen?

Moses was believed to have been a model of compassion; in the Sermon on the Mount, Jesus is likewise presented as a compassionate teacher. But for the time being we should notice not so much what Jesus says as how he says it. Those who listened noticed a different kind of authority in Jesus' voice. They could hear God speaking. It is worth reading the whole sermon for oneself and thinking what makes this way of speaking different. It is certainly challenging, but it is also encouraging. It gives a sense of God's closeness to us, his approachability and tenderness. We can make out Isaiah's signs of the spirit mentioned in Luke 4.

Matthew, like Mark in the preceding passage (Mark 1.22), draws a contrast between Jesus and the scribes. It is a reminder of the difference between a learned study of scripture and one in which we let the power of the text, a divine power, transform our lives.

Teaching a Word of Encouragement

Here are two similar passages.

Matthew 9.35–36

[35]And Jesus went about all the cities and villages, teaching in their synagogues and preaching the gospel of the kingdom, and healing every disease and every infirmity. [36]When he saw the crowds, he had compassion for them, because they were harassed and helpless, like sheep without a shepherd.

Matthew 11.28–30

[28]'Come to me, all who labour and are heavy laden, and I will give you rest. [29]Take my yoke upon you, and learn from me; for I am gentle and lowly in heart, and you will find rest for your souls. [30]For my yoke is easy, and my burden is light.'

How do we listen to these passages? *Lectio divina* **does not need to be arduous. As we learn to listen to Jesus we will find ourselves supported by his compassion; we are invited to discover healing and strength, as well as guidance and a sense of direction. To do so, Jesus offers us his own life and teaching (his 'yoke') as a lesson; and we should learn to read all of scripture as pointing towards him and finding its fulfilment in him.**

Finding a Lonely Place

Jesus can meet people and talk to them in all kinds of places, and in very different ways, depending on the circumstances. We have to be ready to listen to him in more ways than we do to people who preach to us in church – ready to get into a conversation with him, and even to talk back. But we need space and time to be with Jesus. In the Gospels we see Jesus even trying to get away from people to give his disciples a break, even though he feels for the people who have come looking for him and begins to teach them.

Mark 6.30–34

[30]The apostles returned to Jesus, and told him all that they had done and taught. [31]And he said to them, 'Come away by yourselves to a lonely place, and rest a while.' For many were coming and going, and they had no leisure even to eat. [32]And they went away in the boat to a lonely place by themselves. [33]Now many saw them going, and knew them, and they ran there on foot from all the towns, and got there ahead of them. [34]As he went ashore he saw a great throng, and he had compassion on them, because they were like sheep without a shepherd; and he began to teach them many things.

It is important for us to take 'time out' to be with Jesus. This passage is a useful one to gauge the extent to which we are over-committed to our work and engagements: how uncomfortable or envious do we feel as we read it? Do we write it off with a sardonic 'if only!'? And yet we should note that Jesus does give us permission to take the time out that we need to be available as he was for others.

We should also note that it is Jesus, not the disciples, who goes to meet the people who will not leave them alone. Sometimes we simply have to leave demands other people make to him and not suppose that we are the only ones who can be responsible.

For even Jesus made time to find his own spiritual refreshment in prayer to his heavenly Father.

Mark 1.35–38

[35]And in the morning, a great while before day, he rose and went out to a lonely place, and there he prayed. [36]And Simon and those who were with him followed him, [37]and they found him and said to him, 'Everyone is searching for you.' [38]And he said to them, 'Let us go on to the next towns that I may preach there also; for that is why I came.'

The mountains are not only a place of Jesus' public ministry. They are also a desert place where Jesus went out to pray. He had been tempted in the desert (Matthew 4.1), but he overcame the power of Satan and made the desert a place of prayer. It is likewise in finding these desert places that we can begin to hear differently, and discern the divine authority that speaks in the words of the Bible. We do not always have to go out and find them; they come and meet us. The desert places may be any places where we feel lonely, where the ground is rough. But they are places where Jesus has been before. He has made them, potentially, holy places.

We do need places like that. We need to retune our attention to a completely new wavelength; we need to listen to him speaking in our hearts where there is all sorts of interference. Once we have got the tuning right, we can pick up the signals of God's word in all sorts of places, but to start with we will need to learn to be quiet and to learn to listen to the quiet. Jesus is our teacher here.

We can find much comfort in the fact that Jesus had to pray like us and listen to his heavenly Father. He too needed to find the time and place to do so and, no doubt, had to make the time to do so. Like him, we need to learn to listen to God in order to reach out to others with his love, in order to meet people who came from all over the district to find him, let alone go in search of them.

Finding a Blessing

Luke puts Jesus' first sermon on the plain. On the plain Jesus is typically engaged with people in ordinary walks of life and with their own concerns. Luke's context suggests, more than Matthew's, how Jesus is ready to get involved with us in the pressures of ordinary life, and teach us how, in the midst of all that, God is very close. The detail Luke gives of people trying to touch Jesus and find healing puts the sermon in a more crowded setting, crowded both physically and emotionally; it also gives the idea of blessing a more immediate and human impact.

Luke 6.17–20

[17]And he came down with them and stood on a level place, with a great crowd of his disciples and a great multitude of people from all Judea and Jerusalem and the seacoast of Tyre and Sidon, who came to hear him and to be healed of their diseases; [18]and those who were troubled with unclean spirits were cured. [19]And all the crowd sought to touch him, for power came forth from him and healed them all. [20]And he lifted up his eyes on his disciples, and said: 'Blessed are you poor, for yours is the kingdom of God.'

Are we aware of our needs as things that Jesus cares about, things that we can bring to Jesus? When we turn to *lectio divina*, we need to be able to listen to God, which means being ready to set aside our own preoccupations; but we should not be afraid to be honest about our own needs and anxieties, or to share them with God as we listen to the scriptures.

Deep down we often have to revisit the question of how we imagine God to be. Do we think of him as one who blesses, or judges? The two are not exclusive ideas, but we can too easily let our idea of God reinforce our bad ideas of ourselves (or others). Someone once likened the idea of God's blessing to his smiling at us. The psalmist uses the image in Psalm 67, where he lets his face

shine on us. Can we let him look at us and let his face shine on us? Are we ready to learn what his blessing means? Heaven can be found in Charing Cross Road.

Our Hearts Burned within Us

The story of the disciples on the road to Emmaus is an important passage to study in order to understand how *lectio divina* works. It is a very different story from the ones already considered, because it comes after the resurrection; the risen Christ appears unrecognized to two of his disciples. In this story, the disciples are trying to make sense of the death of Jesus and its aftermath. Jesus uses the scriptures to help them understand. He himself has to explain things, and he does so by showing how the scriptures teach them to understand the mystery of his death and resurrection. Jesus shows us who he is through his whole life, but especially through the mystery of his passion, his passing through death to life beyond death. This mystery of Christ's redemption is the key to the Bible. In the course of the conversation Jesus remains hidden from them, but there is a point of disclosure, a moment of contemplation, as it were, where Jesus is recognized for himself in their midst. The moment is a Eucharistic one, reminding us of the centrality of the Eucharist in our awareness of Jesus' living presence. The moment of worship is one where he disappears from their sight again, but at once prompts recognition of his presence with them as they had been reflecting on the scriptures. Their hearts had burned within them. Finally the encounter with Jesus prompts joy and action. They hurry back to Jerusalem and share their experience with the rest of the disciples. *Lectio divina* is a reading of the scriptures that should unite us with the Church, especially in the celebration of the Eucharist.

Luke 24.13–32

[13]That very day two of them were going to a village named Emmaus, about seven miles from Jerusalem [14]and talking with each

other about all these things that had happened. [15]While they were talking and discussing together, Jesus himself drew near and went with them. [16]But their eyes were kept from recognizing him. [17]And he said to them, 'What is this conversation which you are holding with each other as you walk?' And they stood still, looking sad. [18]Then one of them, named Cleopas, answered him, 'Are you the only visitor to Jerusalem who does not know the things that have happened there in these days?' [19]And he said to them, 'What things?' And they said to him, 'Concerning Jesus of Nazareth, who was a prophet mighty in deed and word before God and all the people, [20]and how our chief priests and rulers delivered him up to be condemned to death, and crucified him. [21]But we had hoped that he was the one to redeem Israel. Yes, and besides all this, it is now the third day since this happened. [22]Moreover, some women of our company amazed us. They were at the tomb early in the morning [23]and did not find his body; and they came back saying that they had even seen a vision of angels, who said that he was alive. [24]Some of those who were with us went to the tomb, and found it just as the women had said; but him they did not see.' [25]And he said to them, 'O foolish men, and slow of heart to believe all that the prophets have spoken! [26]Was it not necessary that the Christ should suffer these things and enter into his glory?' [27]And beginning with Moses and all the prophets, he interpreted to them in all the scriptures the things concerning himself. [28]So they drew near to the village to which they were going. He appeared to be going further, [29]but they constrained him, saying, 'Stay with us, for it is toward evening and the day is now far spent.' So he went in to stay with them. [30]When he was at table with them, he took the bread and blessed, and broke it, and gave it to them. [31]And their eyes were opened and they recognized him; and he vanished out of their sight. [32]They said to each other, 'Did not our hearts burn within us while he talked to us on the road, while he opened to us the scriptures?'

The story opens with the disciples talking about what had been going on, trying to make sense of their ordinary experience; above all, in the aftermath of the crucifixion, they were struggling with the question where God was in it all. Again we need to bring these questions to our reading of the scriptures. But we need to let Jesus help us to understand.

He does so in a hidden way, in the way we are guided to use the whole of the scriptures to make sense of the picture. Jesus is not afraid to work with our feelings, especially our feelings of perplexity, sadness, even anger. The story talks about the hopes and fears of the disciples too. All this is relevant to our reflection on scripture.

We need to let our hopes and fears become part of our reading as we strive to understand what God is saying to us. It helps us tune in to the heart, the place where the Holy Spirit is dwelling. The felt response of our inner heart is where we pick up a sense of what Jesus is trying to teach us.

The conversation with the scriptures continues with an invitation to Jesus to stay with them and share their supper. Similarly, the work of reflection needs to turn more personally to Jesus, and to seek to stay with him in prayer. It can be a precious moment of discovery and communion, which is celebrated sacramentally in the Eucharist we share with the whole Christian community.

Practical Section

Rediscovering reading

It may seem strange to have to say something practical about reading. Nowadays, however, reading is far less important as a means of communication than audio-visual media, and this has not made it easier. We expect a message to be visually immediate, easily grasped rather than understood. At the same time there is a huge expansion in the volume of printed words with which we deal, with word-processors, photocopies, email, fax and texting facilities, the mountains of statistical documentation and so on. 'Surfing the net' is the very antithesis of the kind of reading that we need to learn to listen to God. Nowadays, the idea of text has been vulgarized, with the result that we no longer expect to read, but rather to flick through a large proportion of the words we see. We become very cursory; defensive too, seeing how much of the daily postbag can be passed straight into the waste-paper bin. Underneath an avalanche of paper we rarely expect to be on the lookout for a word of life.

At a personal level too we might think how few of our friendships are nowadays maintained by letter rather than by telephone – a real letter, rather than a short postcard, or the word-processed family news bulletin! How ready, then, are we to accept that the written word might be the means of communication between God and mankind, or a source of friendship with him?

If we are readers, we ought to think what we spend most of our time reading, and why, and how. For many of our habits and assumptions about reading need revision when we turn to the scriptures. It is no easy read. For example, they say that there are as many words in a daily paper as in a novel. But it is certainly easier to sit down with a newspaper. In spite of its daily variety, it is the predictability of a paper we enjoy; nothing too threatening, first thing in the day, the stability of the world we are used to! Think how hard it is to start the day with the *Telegraph* rather than the *Guardian*, or vice versa. Headlines, pictures, quips and cartoons, columns, print – everything is intended to make it easy for us to scan, and to feel we are *au courant*, that we can participate coherently, if not intelligently, in the converse of the chattering classes.

And what are our assumptions and expectations about the scriptures? This is something we should consider in our prayer. We must not be surprised if large portions of the Bible disappoint and even infuriate us. We need to pray patiently to learn to listen for what God is trying to say in what we read, rather than what we want to hear; pray too that we will not take its meaning for granted, or be surprised at how it may in fact be inviting us to enter into a dialogue with God. Are we ready to let God teach us how to read the Bible? Can we learn by letting him teach us, through our frustration and puzzlement, the quality of patience and attentiveness that is needed?

An obvious point: we need a Bible we can read without too much practical difficulty in comprehension. There are several modern translations. A scholar can be snooty about their qualities; but we are not trying to be scholars. As readers, and people who pray with the word of God, our needs are different. There is a lot to be said for Bibles that include some guides to reading, as either introductions, section headings, or a few footnotes. Marginal references are a handy way of digging around for parallels; but we must not get sidetracked into just studying references rather than listening to what they are trying to say.

Slow reading

So we have to rediscover the art of reading and be happy to have our reading ability stretched, even to breaking point! In particular we need to learn to read slowly. A much quoted story comes from the *Readers'* *Digest*, which published an article in June 1973 by a businessman, Sidney Piddington, who had been confined three years in a Japanese prisoner of war camp in Singapore. In that time he discovered the 'special joys of super-slow reading' which is the title of the article. Trying to make his precious book last as long as possible, he disciplined himself to linger over each page and enter into the experience being described by the author. His reading fell naturally into the rhythm of listening and responding. As he described it: 'Sometimes just a particular phrase caught my attention, sometimes a sentence. I would read it slowly, analyse it, read it again, perhaps changing down into an even lower gear, and then sit for twenty minutes thinking about it before moving on.' Not only did slowing down make the book last longer, but as a bonus

Piddington discovered that the practice lifted him above the sordidness and senselessness of prison-camp life and put him in a more humane world; super-slow reading preserved his sanity, his human dignity and his inner freedom.

There are many ways of slowing down, besides repeated reading. Early monks learned the text or portions of it by heart; others carefully copied it out. The merit of reading aloud has already been mentioned. Some people like to compare different translations, or parallel passages in the scriptures, and to savour the different slants and emphases that come through. Any of these may serve. I heard of someone who used to write a passage out by heart and then compare what he recalled with the original; both the omissions and the glosses were instructive.

Reflective reading

Reading must also be reflective reading. This is really the subject of the next chapter. Suffice to say here that, as we receive the word of God, we will often find it a help to be able to make connections between our reading and different passages in the scriptures. It is part of the work of understanding to see a passage as part of the scriptures as a whole, which together comprise the word of God. The point here is not cerebration; we are not trying to write an exegesis of the text, or study theology. But sometimes we need to be ready to 'unpack' a passage, and to do so in a way that is theologically responsible (or aware of our theological limitations!): sometimes it will 'unfold' of its own accord, especially when we are more adept at things. In doing so we should feel free to allow our memories (which will be prompted by the Spirit) to guide us in responding to the associations a passage may make in our own minds. A tougher passage, which does not at once lend itself to 'chewing over', may be one to prepare a little more carefully, paying attention to commentaries and studying the words a bit more closely.

The real point in saying this is to counterbalance any exaggeratedly subjective reading of the scriptures. *Lectio divina* will be valueless if we do not engage personally with the scriptures, but we must avoid using them selectively, or only as an echo chamber of our own feelings and thoughts. There is an objectivity to the word of God, an authority, whose meaning we can only understand fully by knowledge of the scriptures as a whole as well as of the way the Church has come to understand them in articulating our faith in Christ. This issue takes us beyond the needs of a beginner: but the point perhaps needs to be made as a caveat against premature complacency about what is involved.

Getting used to biblical literature

The next thing is that we need to drop our expectations of our reading matter. We must let the scriptures unfold themselves and teach us what they are about. That means being patient, and persevering: ideally we should try to read the whole scripture (over a suitable period of time). Only then can we really expect to begin to make sense of the whole thing. That is not to say that we can learn nothing in the meantime. A simple handbook or companion (rather than a commentary) to the Bible may do the trick. It is a difficult story to find one's way in, especially in the Old Testament. Take advantage of what helps. But do not be surprised to find things rather heavy-going, certainly to start with.

The ugliness of language, the obscurity of style and presentation of the message, the remoteness of the story and its cultural setting – all these factors made it scandalously difficult even in the very earliest days of the Church. Even before the New Testament was written, the first apostles, and our Lord himself, had to teach patiently, and not always with much success, that the Old Testament spoke to their world, and that it was the only way really to understand what was going on in Jesus' life.

In the classical and very literary culture of the ancient world reading scripture demanded a major re-orientation to accept the Bible as literature. In our day we are probably in a better position than ever before to appreciate the qualities and power of the biblical narrative. Our difficulties will probably be more with the savagery with which the story of salvation is told; not only human actors do some dreadful things, God too seems rather vindictive. We just have to remember that the authors of the story, over the many centuries of its formation, have only been human, ignorant and sinful. We have a terrible tendency to think God out in our own terms. This is where we must let Jesus teach us to read the Old Testament critically.

The legal cast of so much of the writing will also be rather strange to us: Jesus taught us to understand the function of the Law in a different way, and the early Church realized that the cultic (as opposed to the moral) law of the Old Testament had been superseded by the sacrifice of Christ's death and passion. Again, the New Testament, Hebrews above all, is a valuable teacher for us.

In order to develop a feel for the biblical narrative, whatever sympathy we have for literature will help; especially our ability to engage with the different genres of the various parts of the Bible. A Bible with suitable introductions will help distinguish the various genres. The books of the Law (the Pentateuch) need to be read differently from the historical books that follow, although they seem to be the next chapters in the story. Similarly the prophetic books, which form an immense poetic meditation on the travails of the story of God's people, full of condemnation but also of promise and encouragement. These books are collections of poems composed in different historical settings, and each has been put together with little regard to the original context that often helps us get into them. A Bible with notes and cross-references is a help here, especially to relate them to the contemporary events in the historical books. The 'writings' form the other major category in the Old Testament, including poetry and prose stories, often reflecting the wisdom of later Jewish writers and thinkers.

The New Testament has its genres too. A Gospel is not just a life of Jesus, but presents the good news that he proclaimed: it is a summons to faith. The letters reflect different kinds of relationship between the authors and their recipients, whether whole Church communities or individuals. The Acts of the Apostles needs to be read in conjunction with the Gospel of St Luke, the two books forming a diptych, as the author explains in the prologue to Acts. That leaves the Apocalypse, or Book of Revelation, an exceptional book in the New Testament, and which owes a lot to the apocalyptic imagination of later Jewish literature. It must be understood not as a prediction of the end of the world, but rather as a vision of how the victory of Christ over death is being worked out in the lives of Christians who are still involved in the struggle against sin, and especially those facing martyrdom.

But a literary sense is only an advantage; it is not the point of the exercise. We should still be trying to enter into the story at a different level, to read and hear it as the word of God. Each of us has to find a way of reading that not only works for oneself, but which is also flexible enough to adapt itself to different kinds of scripture. More didactic passages, whether moral or theological (such as in the letters), can speak for themselves more directly; nevertheless, do not forget to bring them into relation to your own life and understanding of Jesus; let them speak to your heart as well as the mind as a call to the continuing work of transformation under grace, which the early Christian tradition saw as an ongoing process of conversion. Gospel passages sometimes need more use of the imagination so as to explore how you 'fit into the story': Jesus is speaking within a human context that we have to make our own. Ignatian meditation often uses this approach, and this is how many people have been introduced to meditating with scripture. It is not necessary always to go to the imaginative lengths some do in responding to such passages: in the end we are trying to listen to the word of God in the Gospel passage. Other narratives, especially in the Old Testament, are much harder to make one's own. Here the emphasis may tend to be on the place of the episode within the epic of salvation history – always remembering to recognize the historical presuppositions which underlie a pre-Christian narrative. Sometimes there is a more or less direct link between it and the Gospel or New Testament writing, a quotation, or an episode which prefigures something in the life of the Lord of the Church.

Sometimes a character will display qualities of faith in the divine promise which is fulfilled in Jesus Christ. Remember Hebrews 11, for example. It is always a help to read the Old Testament in relation to Jesus Christ and to the gospel, however that relation is expressed.

Some perspectives of the Bible story

The story is a huge one but there are underlying themes, and an underlying unity. The writing of the Bible covers a millennium, and the story it tells reaches back a millennium before that. But in the course of it there are perhaps four themes, four ways in which God's word to us comes through, spelling out the way our lives are bound up with his.

First, there is a theme of *covenant* and *promise*. God is with those who belong to him; he leads them and perseveres with them, forgiving them their persistent backsliding. It is a story that repeats itself within the compass of the Old Testament with Israel's recurring periods of faith and distrust, of commitment and disloyalty, of betrayal and the renewal of promise. That story goes on.

Second, there is the theme of *life* or *law*. Law is fundamental to the covenant God makes with his people because he wants us to share his own way of life, and to observe the standards of his faithfulness and justice in the way we live together. His claim on us is as absolute as his own graciousness and mercy in meeting our own faltering efforts to respond to it. The wisdom literature of the Old Testament is a variation on this theme.

Third, there is the theme of *prophecy* in which God continues to call people to himself and to make them responsible for his own work in leading his people. This is a word both of vocation and of mission. We are ourselves entrusted with his word and endowed with the spirit as bearers of it, a word calling his people to conversion, a word of healing and encouragement, a word of consolation.

Fourth, there is the theme of *judgement*, a word which distinguishes between good and evil, one which puts all things in a perspective of divine judgement, standing them against the horizon of the end of the world, and which summons us to work now for the kingdom of God, which will have no end, where God alone will be Lord.

These four themes run through both the Old and the New Testaments. They help us to tune in to the underlying unity of the biblical story as the story of our salvation in Christ. They are particularly prominent in the Old Testament, where we can see how human feelings and reactions, how all sorts of human character are lived out, one way and another towards God, and how God can take human life and change it for his purpose, and make it a vehicle of his grace and love. In this way we can begin to see how this vast story is to be understood as a story of faith, and as one that finds its completion in the birth of Our Lord. The Old Testament prepares the way for the New: it is the story of how room is made in our midst for the incarnation of our God.

In this way then we can begin to find Jesus as an abiding presence throughout the scriptures. For a Christian, the heart of the scriptures is Jesus' own word to us, the Gospel, which he entrusts to us for the salvation of all. The story of Jesus, told four times over in the New Testament, is central to our grasp of the divine meaning of all the scriptures. As both God and man he not only is the key to the message, he teaches us how to respond to God's constant invitation to turn to him. Jesus was the one perfectly faithful to God, the one who, even in Gethsemane and on Calvary, did not lose faith or hope in him; he is no less our companion and unfailing guide. As the one who was perfectly just and without sin, he is for us the author of justice and the way of true life. As the one utterly obedient in his response to God's call, he calls us to his service and entrusts us with his own mission. In his wisdom he teaches us to see truly the difference between good and evil, and he, through whom all things were made in wisdom and beauty, is himself for us the author of new and everlasting life.

As we find our way around the whole of this story, we can also begin to find the way it links into the story of our own lives. We are part of the story. But it is more than a grand design in which we are invited to play our part. We can learn from the way God has taken the initiative with people to look for him in our own lives, and there is much to learn from the various ways others have responded to him. That is how we learn how to live in relation to God.

Chapter Two:
Receiving the Word

The traditional name for the second movement in *lectio divina* is meditation. This is again a little misleading as the term was used to mean something rather specific in the monastic tradition from which the theory of *lectio divina* derives, and since the Middle Ages the term has come to be used in very different ways.

Not many years ago, 'meditation' would have been understood to mean a fairly methodical reflection on a text of the Bible or a theme, in which the imagination was usually heavily engaged. The intention behind this activity was to discover, through the establishment of some personal rapport with the text, points for consideration, something that would help come to some conclusions about a person's life and, usually, about God's will for it. A critical commentator of this kind of meditation compared it to a butcher's work, cutting dead meat into joints ready for cooking! The real difference between this kind of meditation and that intended in *lectio divina* is that it cultivates a rapport only with the text; it is not about deepening personal contact with the word of God.

More recently, perhaps especially under the influence of people's interest in Eastern religious wisdom, meditation has been understood as a technique of mental practice, in one way or another transcending the normal processes of rational thought in favour of some less differentiated state of consciousness; transcendental meditation was a fashionable example some years ago. Although the influences on this sense of meditation have come from oriental religions, there is a little understood Christian tradition of prayer in this style too. I expect that most people will understand the term nowadays in this sense, and it is rightly becoming increasingly common; but it is not what we need to explore here, in as much as it does not involve reflection on a text such as we try to do in *lectio divina* in order to listen to God.

There is a danger, too, that the meditation we explore in *lectio divina* is rather narrowly understood in the sense it has in the kind of mantra prayer that is referred to, for instance, in the medieval mystical text *The Cloud of Unknowing*. Centering Prayer is one of the names for the process that has encouraged this kind of work with scriptural texts. In this kind of prayer the word is not the focus of the work that a person is engaged in; the word is just a way of keeping the rational mind quiet while the heart is turned to God. In a mantra prayer the word is only incidental, whereas in *lectio divina* the word or words are the key that unlocks the path inwards to the heart, to prayer and contemplation. That said, however, the word that has served its purpose in meditation can be an anchor in the work of prayer and contemplation. But that is later on, developing out of the movement we are considering now, traditionally called meditation.

In *lectio divina*, meditation means something quite simple: it is receiving and taking to heart a word that I believe is personally addressed to me. As I begin to enter into scripture by prayerful reading and as I begin to hear the word of God, I listen and incline the ear of my heart to it. I treasure it, and ponder on it, seeking to understand and respond to what I begin to understand God is saying to me. In a sense, this kind of meditation is the point at which *lectio divina* takes off, because when we let scripture sink into us it becomes a word of life. We need to let it sink into our hearts as much as into our heads. What we read are no longer just words on a page, or a story, edifying or otherwise; we have begun to tune in to something else. We are beginning to pick up God's way of addressing me, his way of breathing life into my being. That is why it involves our hearts more than our heads; it is not just informing our minds, it is shaping our lives. If we are receiving the word in this sense, we are trying to catch the breath with which it is uttered; we are breathing in the Holy Spirit with which God utters his word; and, in our hearts, it is the Holy Spirit with which our own spirit resonates when we hear the scripture as word of God. For us that Spirit is the breath of life.

This makes meditation sound rather complicated; in fact it is quite simple, but very profound. At its simplest it is a two-stage process: repetition of the words, and digesting them, taking them into oneself. In the ancient world reading was not a silent activity. One or two famously learned men, like St Ambrose of Milan, impressed their contemporaries because they used to read without making any sound. But normally people talked their reading over to themselves. *Meditari* was the verb used for the murmuring activity of reading. In Latin, *meditari* covers a range of meanings. Its classical meaning meant generally to reflect on something, to ponder on it, without necessarily any spiritual import. It also meant to practise something, especially to practise a speech one was about to deliver, to rehearse one's lines. In this sense, St Benedict uses the word to describe what monks who do not yet know the psalms or Office readings by heart should do during the hours between Vigils and dawn in winter (Rule of St Benedict 8, 3). Novices especially had a lot to 'meditate' and the Novitiate they lived in was set aside for them to do so (Rule 58, 5). St Benedict was conscious how one person's meditation might distract another person who was trying to take a nap!

Repetition is only the first stage of the process. Meditation is also a way of absorbing a text, of appropriating it and of being changed by it at a personal level. In contrast to the modern antipathy to 'rote' learning, the ancient world believed that real learning was learning by heart, but also that learning by heart actually did enable the heart to be engaged and to integrate what was learned into a person's way of life. So reading had to be broken into its parts, analysed, and understood in relation to the entire body of previously acquired learning. Memory was regarded as a far richer dimension of our personality than is usual now, in spite of psychoanalysis. Entrusting something to one's memory enabled it to be absorbed into a person's character at an interior level. Learning became a source of wisdom.

An unlikely image used for this was that of cows chewing their fodder. But it is a good image. The image of cows making milk catches the truth that the words of scripture need digestion, not only with our heads but by the whole system, like cows chewing, digesting and then chewing the cud as the food is turned into milk. The metaphor underlies the modern sense of rumination. Sometimes the roughage needs a lot of digestion, but that milk is the food we need for our souls.

In order to let this happen, we often have to enter into the meaning of what we read. We can try to enter into the story in a personal kind of way, looking for how that story matches up to and sheds light on our own story. Meditation on a passage tries to open it up so that we can find in our own lives the same spirit, the same hope and life on which we ponder in our reading. The biblical witness to faith helps to shape our own story of faith. Meditation is a two-way process – God's addressing us, as well as our getting into the story – but the fundamental thing is our hearing and receiving what we hear as a word of life. That is what creates the bond between God and us that makes prayer possible and which enables us to live in faith.

On the Lips and in the Heart

In meditation all we are trying to do is to dwell on a word or a passage in our reading that has some resonance with us. By quietly repeating a phrase, ruminating on it, we turn it over in our mind so that its meaning enters into our heart. The word moves, as it were, from our ears or lips to our mind and into our heart. Paul, drawing on a beautiful passage in the Old Testament (Deuteronomy 30.4), makes the link.

Romans 10.4–8
[4]For Christ is the end of the law, that every one who has faith may be justified. [5]Moses writes that the one who practises the

righteousness which is based on the law shall live by it.[6] But the righteousness based on faith says, Do not say in your heart, 'Who will ascend into heaven?' (that is, to bring Christ down) [7]or 'Who will descend into the abyss?' (that is, to bring Christ up from the dead). [8]But what does it say? The word is near you, on your lips and in your heart (that is, the word of faith which we preach).

This passage in Romans is a good example of the way that the Christian community used the Old Testament from an early stage of its history. Here the interpretation focuses the understanding and closeness of the word on Jesus Christ himself: incarnate and risen to new life, his words are alive and active. St Paul, writing before the formation of the New Testament, refers to the preaching of the Church; but the word of God is alive and active in our own reading of the scriptures in the public and private prayer of the Church.

In *lectio divina* it is always worth taking the original context of an Old Testament allusion into consideration. In the original context of this passage, in Deuteronomy, Moses is addressing Israel at the end of their journey through the desert before his own death and their entrance into the Promised Land; he is inviting them to enter into God's covenant, conscious of God's faithfulness to Israel. This context helps us see that the faith, which is all-important to Paul's argument in Romans and which grounds our commitment to God, stems from his faithfulness to us. And this two-way commitment of faith centres on Jesus.

The word that Jesus speaks is for us a new covenant, the basis of a new relationship with God, the word that we listen to in *lectio divina*. The connection made here between lips and heart reminds us of God's closeness to us when we feed on the scriptures, just as much as it teaches us the need to take the word of God deeply into our heart.

46

A similar passage earlier on in Deuteronomy was referred to by Christ himself in summarizing the Law (Matthew 22.37).

Deuteronomy 6.4–9

[4]'Hear, O Israel: The LORD our God is one LORD; [5]and you shall love the LORD your God with all your heart, and with all your soul, and with all your might. [6]And these words which I command you this day shall be upon your heart; [7]and you shall teach them diligently to your children, and shall talk of them when you sit in your house, and when you walk by the way, and when you lie down, and when you rise. [8]And you shall bind them as a sign upon your hand, and they shall be as frontlets between your eyes. [9]And you shall write them on the doorposts of your house and on your gates.'

Again the link is made between an internal and external appropriation of the word. The two go together, and in particular the point is made here that the exterior repetition of the word is a precious way of learning and remembering it. That is how it can shape a way of life. Not only are the texts a sign of the covenant made, but also a way of remembering it so as to live by it.

The precept was taken literally by the Jews of Jesus' day, although Jesus warned against a merely formal observance, where things were done only to be seen by other people (Matthew 23.5). For exterior and interior do not always go together, and formal observance needs to be internalized. The Gospels refer to the old prophetic warnings about a split between external performance and the heart's focus on God (Matthew 15.8). The importance of internalizing the word is something the practice of *meditatio* takes very seriously indeed.

The Psalms give several examples of the Jewish understanding of meditation that *lectio divina* is based on. Psalm 119, the longest psalm, which is a meditation on the law of God as the rule of a good life, contains many references about the value of repetition as a way of taking God's word to heart.

Psalm 119.11–16

[11] I have laid up your word in my heart, that I might not sin against you.

[12] Blessed are you, O LORD; teach me your statutes!

[13] With my lips I declare all the ordinances of your mouth.

[14] In the way of your testimonies I delight as much as in all riches.

[15] I will meditate on your precepts, and fix my eyes on your ways.

[16] I will delight in your statutes; I will not forget your word.

These verses suggest that meditation on God's word is part of a complex process of appropriation at every level of one's being. They mention eyes and mouth, as well as meditation, remembering and delight. The balance, characteristic of the style of Hebrew psalmody, is made between laying up in the heart and declaring with the lips; and later on between the complementary levels of attention with the eyes and with the mind in meditation.

A similar passage may be found in verses 43–48, where a balance is struck between the word in the mouth and the meditation of the heart.

Sweeter than Honey

Meditation in this kind of way teaches us how to delight in the scriptures. They are not immediately accessible, but with patience and developing familiarity they can become a source of refreshment. Psalm 19 speaks of them as sweeter than honey – the same image is used in Psalm 119.103. The word of God is not just stolid bread and butter! But we cannot expect to get a taste for scripture without taking trouble with it.

Psalm 19.7–14

[7]The law of the LORD is perfect, reviving the soul;

the testimony of the LORD is sure, making wise the simple;

[8]the precepts of the LORD are right, rejoicing the heart;

the commandment of the LORD is pure, enlightening the eyes;

[9]the fear of the LORD is clean, enduring for ever;

the ordinances of the LORD are true, and righteous altogether.

[10]More to be desired are they than gold, even much fine gold;

sweeter also than honey and drippings of the honeycomb.

[11]Moreover by them is your servant warned;

in keeping them there is great reward.

[12]But who can discern his errors? Make me clear from hidden faults.

[13]Keep back your servant also from presumptuous sins;

let them not have dominion over me!

Then I shall be blameless, and innocent of great transgression.

[14]Let the words of my mouth and the meditation of my heart be

acceptable in your sight, O LORD, my rock and my redeemer.

The passage is an eloquent testimony to the value of a faithful reading of scripture. Perhaps we can use it as a prayer by turning the statements into requests: may it revive my soul, may it make me wise ...

The metaphor of honey is directly related to the imagery of chewing and digestion that became central to the Christian understanding of *meditatio* we mentioned in the introduction to this chapter.

Sweet to the Mouth but Bitter to the Stomach

The word that is sweet in the mouth needs to be chewed and digested. Receiving the word of God is a process of nourishment, where the word of God gives life to the one who obeys. There are a couple of places where the Bible talks of eating the scroll on which God's word has been written. The first is the prophet Ezekiel (Ezekiel 3.1–3), and the motif was taken up in the New Testament in Revelation.

Revelation 10.9–11

[9]So I went to the angel and told him to give me the little scroll; and he said to me, 'Take it and eat; it will be bitter to your stomach, but sweet as honey in your mouth.' [10]And I took the little scroll from the hand of the angel and ate it; it was sweet as honey in my mouth, but when I had eaten it my stomach was made bitter. [11]And I was told, 'You must again prophesy about many peoples and nations and tongues and kings.'

It would probably be intolerable if the scriptures only tasted of honey! But this is a sobering reminder that the word of God is not just easy talk or words of comfort. The bitterness of the scroll is because of the toughness of the message as well as the seriousness of the commission entrusted to its recipients.

We can recall that it is through learning to delight in God's word that we will discover his purposes for us. What we read is not always immediately attractive, but it will help to start by paying attention to what we do find attractive; gradually increasing familiarity with God's way of talking will make our palate more sensitive to the full range in his style.

Meditation may begin with enjoying our reading. That is not a bad idea; it is a response that helps us open ourselves fully to its meaning. But we have to move on from mere enjoyment and start to use our reading to do work on ourselves. Taking the word to heart and turning our hearts to God is more demanding than just sitting back after a good meal.

Soil of the Heart

If meditation starts with repetition of God's word, it is completed by taking it to heart. The scriptures offer us a completely different set of images to consider what this involves. The imagery is that of the seed and the soil in which it is sown and takes root. This time the imagery helps us to think more profoundly about the way we listen to and receive God's word.

Several times in the Gospel Jesus is reported as saying 'If you have ears, listen'. But the very fact that he said this shows people actually found it hard to listen in the relevant sense. The problems we have listening to Jesus are introduced in the Parable of the Sower. The Gospels themselves give the interpretation. The word is like a seed; the ground receives it, it germinates, grows and bears fruit. The story is already teaching us something: to listen we need to be like soil receiving seed. The words we read are living things, or words that will come to life in us. They are not just words on a page either; they are sown. Luke is explicit. The seed is the word of God. In some sense our reading opens us up to God's work of sowing his seed in our hearts. Or it can do. There are, however, many things that get in the way.

Luke 8.11–15

[11]'Now the parable is this: The seed is the word of God. [12]The ones along the path are those who have heard; then the devil comes and takes away the word from their hearts, that they may not believe and be saved. [13]And the ones on the rock are those who, when they hear the word, receive it with joy; but these have no root, they believe for a while and in time of temptation fall away. [14]And as for what fell among the thorns, they are those who hear, but as they go on their way they are choked by the cares and riches and pleasures of life, and their fruit does not mature. [15]And as for that in the good soil, they are those who, hearing the word, hold it fast in an honest and good heart, and bring forth fruit with patience.'

Three different kinds of obstacles are mentioned. In the first case, the words cannot even 'germinate'. These are the fundamental difficulties we have with attention, letting what we read even register with us. The specific problem here noted by the Gospels is more serious: the devil comes and takes the word away. We have to live with our weakness when it comes to the difficulty of paying attention to God. But there is a far worse problem when we simply do not want to listen to him at all. Sometimes we have to face up to the fundamental attitudes of sin that prevent us listening to God. Luke goes on to say that the devil takes the word away 'in case they should believe and be saved'. This is a reminder that all listening to God is part of an attitude of faith, a sense of need as well as of trust and hope. We may need to pray for a clearer sense of this faith when we begin to listen to the scriptures prayerfully.

The second kind of obstacle is the poverty of our own listening. We respond quickly, but the seed cannot take root in our lives. The soil is too shallow. In a time of trial we give up. The Greek word used here for 'time of temptation' means more than temptation in the ordinary sense – they are the thorns which Jesus goes on to mention: it means a time of trial serious enough to shake our faith as a whole. Jesus distinguishes between an immediate response at an emotional level and the quality of our commitment, a steadiness of purpose which resides in our wills. Not that we should not listen to him with joy – or with any other feeling – but the fruitfulness of our listening will be measured not by our feelings but by our lives. It is important to be clear about this distinction in our reading and listening. We certainly make a fundamental mistake if we read for the sake of some emotional state: our motive should be a search for truth and wisdom. That can transform our lives.

The final problem arises from our preoccupations: the worries, as well as the riches and pleasures of life – the two kinds of problem are related to each other. Mark and Matthew both mention the way we are taken in and deceived by wealth; and Mark focuses on desires rather than pleasures – the way we hanker after things, which is a wider category than just pleasure. However it is expressed, the key problem here arises from a lack of simplicity and integrity in our lives. The seed of God's word takes root and grows, but it is choked by all the other plants competing in the 'ecosystem' of our life.

These are different kinds of obstacle. The good news is that to a great extent it is by trying to listen to the word and take it into our lives that we become more clearly aware of the various things that get in the way. The word teaches us the kind of work we need to do on ourselves in order to listen better. The one who sows the seed also prepares the ground and helps us to improve the soil.

The good soil is one where we are uncluttered enough to listen and receive the word (as Mark tells the parable), hold it and make it part of our lives and let it bear fruit. Luke brings out the need for patience or steadfastness. We cannot and should not expect quick results. The fruit of *lectio divina* needs a long time to ripen. In particular the word teaches us that the difficulties we have to face in holding the word and making it part of our lives also help us do so more fruitfully.

Ears to Hear

The Parable of the Sower, the first parable in all the Gospels' accounts of Jesus' teaching, deals with some of the problems we have hearing God. But what do we listen out for when we are trying to receive God's word? Sometimes Jesus' teaching is clear; but the heart of his teaching was in the parables, and perhaps one thing our *meditatio* can try to do is to see our lives and the world as parables in the same kind of way. The key to a parable is that it conveys a hint, a point of insight into the

Kingdom of God, the new order of things that God is bringing into existence. We do well, I think, to try to learn to see our lives as stories in the same kind of way. Another thing about parables is that they often have some kind of paradox or impossibility at the heart of the picture. These paradoxes are the point at which the Kingdom of God may be glimpsed. If we look at our lives as parables we should pay particular attention to the areas where we sense tension, or impossibility, places where we are sure our own resources fail; that may be the point where God's meaning for us may be pressing in. Inevitably we will need to take a lot of time to find the positive meaning in the paradoxes and contradictions of life; but that is how the parables generally work.

Mark 4.9

[9]And he said, 'He who has ears to hear, let him hear.'

The comment is recorded several times in the Gospels. It is characteristic of human beings to have the experience but miss the meaning, especially if we are on unfamiliar ground. All the more important to be especially attentive to God's meaning, which is always unfamiliar to those who have not begun to learn how to listen. That is why it is important to deepen our capacity to receive God's word, as the Parable of the Sower illustrated.

However, we are not entirely dependent on our own resources. Jesus helps us, as he helped his disciples, to understand.

Mark 4.33–34

[33]With many such parables he spoke the word to them, as they were able to hear it; [34]he did not speak to them without a parable, but privately to his own disciples he explained everything.

At the heart of the Gospel is a secret, a mystery of the Kingdom, which is not possible for everybody to understand, but which holds the key to the meaning of our life. God's meaning is not

easy to follow – but Jesus helps us to understand. Just as he explained everything to his disciples, meditation is giving Jesus time to help us understand God's meaning.

How can Jesus do this for us? That we must leave to him and to the way he touches us in the depths of our hearts. One way, I think, that helps us open up the meaning of a passage we are reflecting on is to consider the way it brings to mind other passages of the scripture, as well as helps us make connections between what we read and our experience. That is why meditation ought to be fairly leisurely and without fixed techniques and schemes. It must be open to the Spirit; and attentive to Jesus, and what he may be leading us to discover.

What we need to be on the lookout for are points of insight. Always prefer insights into yourself to those into others: growth in wisdom, which is the work of the Spirit, is never won through blaming others; it always includes ourselves. Insight can come suddenly, like a flash of light, or gradually as a dawning in our minds. Sometimes it is less striking, more like the clearing of mist.

Matthew 13.13–16

[13]'This is why I speak to them in parables, because seeing they do not see, and hearing they do not hear, nor do they understand. [14]With them indeed is fulfilled the prophecy of Isaiah which says: "You shall indeed hear but never understand, and you shall indeed see but never perceive. [15]For this people's heart has grown dull, and their ears are heavy of hearing, and their eyes they have closed, lest they should perceive with their eyes, and hear with their ears, and understand with their heart, and turn for me to heal them." [16]But blessed are your eyes, for they see, and your ears, for they hear.'

Listening does not automatically mean understanding. Understanding is not a matter only of intellectual insight: it is a matter of the heart. To understand God's word we need to want to be changed and to be healed by him. We have to learn to acknowledge the sickness that disables our perception, which coarsens our hearts and makes us shy away from the light. Again it is the words we read which can help us here: scripture can help a diagnosis as well as provide a therapy for our hearts. Finding Jesus is always a source of blessing.

Luke 8.16–18

[16]'No one after lighting a lamp covers it with a vessel, or puts it under a bed, but puts it on a stand, that those who enter may see the light. [17]For nothing is hid that shall not be made manifest, nor anything secret that shall not be known and come to light. [18]Take heed then how you hear; for to the one who has will more be given, and from the one who has not, even what they think that they have will be taken away.'

The words we tune into can become a light that discloses the hidden corners of the heart. Meditation helps penetrate our hardness of heart. It opens up a place of prayer, a place of vision.

Jesus sounds rather bleak in the last verse. In the context of *lectio divina* the point is rather obvious. If we can begin to listen to God in our meditation we will be able to learn what he has to say to us personally; and that goes beyond the mere words we start with.

Taking the Word to Heart

Like any great literature, the word of God does not have a simple message for us to 'get' and then move on to the next one. Its meaning is something we will discover unfolding as it becomes an integral part of our spiritual imagination. Often, then, it is enough in meditation to be able to store the word of God in our hearts, and to cultivate the qualities of heart that will let us keep the word well. The time will come, in God's good time, when we can return to the word we have meditated on and understand. More likely, it will stir in our memories and bring us to understand.

The Sermon on the Mount (Matthew 5–7), in particular, teaches a number of lessons on how to take the word to heart. Jesus talks about internalizing the message in a radical way.

Matthew 5.20–24, 43–48

[20]'For I tell you, unless your righteousness exceeds that of the scribes and Pharisees, you will never enter the kingdom of heaven. [21]You have heard that it was said to people of old, "You shall not kill; and whoever kills shall be liable to judgment." [22]But I say to you that every one who is angry with a fellow human being shall be liable to judgment; whoever insults him or her shall be liable to the council, and whoever says, "You fool!" shall be liable to the hell of fire. [23]So if you are offering your gift at the altar, and there remember that a fellow human being has something against you, [24] leave your gift there before the altar and go; first be reconciled to him or her, and then come and offer your gift. . . .'

[43]'You have heard that it was said, "You shall love your neighbour and hate your enemy." [44]But I say to you, Love your enemies and pray for those who persecute you, [45]so that you may be children of your Father who is in heaven; for he makes his sun rise on the evil and on the good, and sends rain on the just and on the unjust. [46]For if you love those who love you, what reward have you? Do not even the tax collectors do the same? [47]And if you salute only your own kin, what more are you doing than others? Do not even the Gentiles do the same? [48]You, therefore, must be perfect, as your heavenly Father is perfect.'

Jesus teaches us to apply the words of the Old Testament in a radical and interior way: to examine our thoughts and desires.

We can generally adapt the dialectic pattern Jesus uses to sharpen our own listening: 'You have heard how it was said ... but I say to you ...'

This kind of self-examination is only morbid if there is no faith in God and no hope in his power to heal and transform. But the perfection Jesus refers to is not the self-perfection of the vain; it is our maturity as God's children, in whom God's word is bearing a generous harvest.

Discerning the Intentions of the Heart

Another way of taking the word of God to heart is to tune in to ourselves as we listen and take note of our feelings. This 'felt response' is one that comes from a place deeper than our head. For instance, we need to pay attention not only to what Jesus says – don't get angry; love your enemies, or whatever – but also to the way we feel when we hear that. That gives me a chance to consider my feelings before God. I may feel that anger is justified; but I have never felt able to express it properly. That is an extreme example (but perhaps not uncommon). But in such a case, it might prompt a prayer for courage, or wisdom to know how to use the anger constructively rather than self-destructively. I expect that more often we may be drawn to reflect on our fears, our anxieties, lack of hope or things like that. The importance of this approach for me is that it is a precious way of getting into the heart. The heart is our personal centre, and although it is deeper than our emotional life, our felt response to things is a good way of finding a path to the door. Within is the place where we can be quietly with God in prayer.

The passage that best shows an appreciation of how the word of God helps as a diagnosis of our thoughts and the hidden movements of the heart is in the Letter to the Hebrews.

Hebrews 4.12–16

[12]For the word of God is living and active, sharper than any two-edged sword, piercing to the division of soul and spirit, of joints and marrow, and discerning the thoughts and intentions of the heart. [13]And before him no creature is hidden, but all are open and laid bare to the eyes of him with whom we have to do.

[14]Since therefore we have a great high priest who has passed through the heavens, Jesus the Son of God, let us hold fast to our confession. [15]For we have not a high priest who is unable to sympathize with our weaknesses but one who in every way has been tempted as we are, yet without sinning. [16]Let us then with confidence draw near to the throne of grace, that we may receive mercy and find grace to help us in time of need.

In this process of reflection we have been considering as *meditatio*, we are seeking to enter into the word of the scriptures we have read. It means entering into our own response to it (positive and negative), not only at the level of the head, but also (more importantly) at the level of the heart. All prayer involves a pilgrimage from the head to the heart, a journey inwards. To start with our feelings runs the danger of emotionalism or sentimentality; but not to notice one's feelings, or to avoid a response to the scripture which brings them into play, will prevent the word of scripture from reaching our heart and thus prevent its becoming there a word of God for us. For although feelings are not the same as the heart, they show us the way towards it. The heart is a secret place largely hidden from us, a holy place where we bear the image of God because it is where God dwells. The word of God helps us enter into that holy place and releases there its power to recreate us through our engagement through the Spirit with the Father who is revealed in the Son.

Word of Healing

The word of God is not only a means of diagnosis; it is also a source of healing, a therapy of the soul. Exposure to the spirit in the spiritual world promotes healing in the human world. It is, as always, a gradual process. One way in which it happens is that hope breaks a log-jam and helps get things moving.

Any of the stories of healing in the Bible can serve here.

Luke 4.40–41

[40]Now when the sun was setting, all those who had any that were sick with various diseases brought them to him; and he laid his hands on every one of them and healed them. [41]And demons also came out of many, crying, 'You are the Son of God!' But he rebuked them, and would not allow them to speak, because they knew that he was the Christ.

The important thing is that we have to accept our need for healing.

Luke 8.43–48

[43]And a woman who had had a flow of blood for twelve years and could not be healed by any one, [44]came up behind him, and touched the fringe of his garment; and immediately her flow of blood ceased. [45]And Jesus said, 'Who was it that touched me?' When all denied it, Peter said, 'Master, the multitudes surround you and press upon you!' [46]But Jesus said, 'Some one touched me; for I perceive that power has gone forth from me.' [47]And when the woman saw that she was not hidden, she came trembling, and falling down before him declared in the presence of all the people why she had touched him, and how she had been immediately healed. [48]And he said to her, 'Daughter, your faith has made you well; go in peace.'

The beautiful thing in this story is how Jesus establishes the personal contact with the woman. She is desperate, diffident of going up to Jesus herself: Mark's version adds the detail, 'If only I can touch the hem of his garment I will be well'. Her faith, hesitant of a personal encounter, was justified, but it was not enough for Jesus. He takes the initiative and looks for her. There is so much in this story that lends itself to meditation.

A Pure Heart

The goal of this process of *meditatio* is the development of a kind of transparency, where we are able to be utterly open to God, sensitive and responsive to his word. Traditionally this transparency was called 'purity of heart', which certainly meant a great deal more than freedom from sexual 'impurity' in more recent Christian jargon. For the monastic tradition it meant the achievement of human freedom, pure and simple, free from any of the plethora of dependencies and interferences that diminish a human being. It is a transparency in the sense that we know that we are seen and known by God, even as we hope to see and know him. It brings a continual awareness of God's presence in our hearts.

It is the goal of a lifetime's growth to Christian maturity. To reach it means being ready to deal with the manifold impurity that bedevils our inner life.

Mark 7.6–7, 18–23

[6]And he said to them, 'Well did Isaiah prophesy of you hypocrites, as it is written, "This people honours me with their lips, but their heart is far from me; [7]in vain do they worship me, teaching as doctrines the precepts of men".' . . .

[18]And he said to them, 'Then are you also without understanding? Do you not see that whatever goes into someone from outside cannot cause defilement, [19]since it enters, not the heart but the stomach, and so passes on?' (Thus he declared all foods clean.) [20]And

he said, 'What comes out of a person is what causes defilement. [21]For from within, out of the human heart, come evil thoughts, fornication, theft, murder, adultery, [22]coveting, wickedness, deceit, licentiousness, envy, slander, pride, foolishness. [23]All these evil things come from within, and they cause defilement.'

The discussion here turns on Jesus' attitude to the complex food laws contained in the Old Testament. It is an example of how Jesus teaches us to interpret the Old Testament: he does not say that the Law of Moses is irrelevant; but it is not enough to stay at the external level. Morally and spiritually, what goes into the mouth is not as important as what comes out of the mouth. Interestingly the Gospel writer glosses the words of Jesus with a remark to justify the later Christian dispensation from these laws.

The contrast here is extended to the contrast between words that remain only on the lips and those that come from within our hearts. Jesus is criticizing the traditional teaching of the Pharisees; but the teaching is based on a superficial reading of the scriptures rather than one where the words have been taken into the heart. The authority of Jesus' own teaching struck people because it was different. It got them in a different place, addressed them in their real selves and helped them be changed. But this sobering passage highlights some of the kinds of desire that, like the thorns in the Parable of the Sower, compete for space with the word of God in our hearts. They are the kinds of thing that choke the path to the heart.

The clearest of Jesus' teaching about the pure heart is in the Beatitudes.

Matthew 5.1–12
[1]Seeing the crowds, he went up on the mountain, and when he sat down his disciples came to him. [2]And he opened his mouth and

taught them, saying: [3]'Blessed are the poor in spirit, for theirs is the kingdom of heaven. [4]Blessed are those who mourn, for they shall be comforted. [5]Blessed are the meek, for they shall inherit the earth. [6]Blessed are those who hunger and thirst for righteousness, for they shall be satisfied. [7]Blessed are the merciful, for they shall obtain mercy. [8]Blessed are the pure in heart, for they shall see God. [9]Blessed are the peacemakers, for they shall be called children of God. [10]Blessed are those who are persecuted for righteousness' sake, for theirs is the kingdom of heaven. [11]Blessed are you when people revile you and persecute you and utter all kinds of evil against you falsely on my account. [12]Rejoice and be glad, for your reward is great in heaven, for so they persecuted the prophets who were before you.'

The people Jesus calls blessed or happy are so because they are the natural constituents of God's new world, his Kingdom. What makes them happy is a list of things we might not rate so highly as keys to happiness, but they are what make it possible to belong to the Kingdom: poverty of spirit (simplicity, an undivided heart), gentleness, compassion (the ability to mourn), hunger and thirst for right, mercy (as well as justice), purity of heart. They are the fruit of humility – good fruit too, for they make it possible for people to live together peacefully. Pope Paul VI spoke memorably of Christians' being called to build a civilization of love: these qualities are the building bricks of such a civilization.

They are things that we should try to rate more highly, then, if we do hope for a better future. But they go against the grain, and they do not flourish unopposed, as Jesus warns us when he calls the last group of people happy who are persecuted in the cause of right. Consider what they are up against. The opposites: (indulgence of spirit) greed, hard-heartedness, contempt, (hunger and thirst for ... things?) materialism, injustice (let

alone mercy), impurity of heart, violence and persecution, taking it out on others. These are the de-civilizers; they are very powerful forces at work around us, and within us.

That is why Jesus is the key to our hope. The life of the Beatitudes is one we learn from him, in friendship with him. The Beatitudes and other passages like them pick out some of the kinds of people who are likely to find this insight into Christ – and the reality of his Kingdom – easiest to attain. They are people who cannot live on their own emotional or personal resources, but for that reason look for everything to God.

Storing the Word up in the Heart

Finally we ought not to leave this long series of reflections on receiving the word without paying attention to Mary, the mother of Jesus. For, especially in the Gospel of St Luke, she is presented as a model of listening.

Luke 2.16–20

[16]And they went with haste, and found Mary and Joseph, and the babe lying in a manger. [17]And when they saw it they made known the saying which had been told them concerning this child; [18]and all who heard it wondered at what the shepherds told them. [19]But Mary kept all these things, pondering them in her heart. [20]And the shepherds returned, glorifying and praising God for all they had heard and seen, as it had been told them.

An intriguing variation of the story we noted in the Introduction, when Mary and the family thought Jesus was mad, is given in Luke (Luke 8.19–21). The reason for their arrival is omitted and so Jesus' definition of his real family is no longer a snub, but becomes one that can include his human mother, whom we have seen took particular care 'to hear the word of God and do it'. For when the angel Gabriel brought the news of God's plan for the incarnation, she replied: 'Be it done to me according to your word.'

By the same token, Mary is shown in the Acts of the Apostles as devoted to prayer.

Acts 1.14

[14]All these with one accord devoted themselves to prayer, together with the women and Mary the mother of Jesus, and with his brothers.

Practical Section

A simple suggestion

So how do we meditate on scripture? The main point is that we try to find a way, however and whatever we read, to let our reading speak for itself and sink in at a personal level as something in which we are involved, and which does speak to us. As was suggested in the first chapter, the simplest approach is to read slowly enough to be able to pick up when and where a sentence or phrase speaks to us. Then we can simply stop and repeat it to ourselves carefully and often enough to let its meaning sink in. Meditation goes hand in hand with the right kind of reading; we must take it slowly and reflectively, and be ready to let our meditation set the pace and approach in our reading. We can let the word we are listening to help shape our thinking about ourselves, other people or God; a dialogue between ourselves and the word we are tuning into can then begin, where we talk over things (not necessarily in words or even thoughts!) in response to the word we have received. In so far as we have tuned in to God's word and are responding to him, our words or thoughts will be words of prayer. We may not, however, think of it like that, but that means we are learning to pray in a new way, which can at least enrich the way we might be used to praying.

A longer suggestion to help get started

We need to remember to quieten down before starting to read. This was described in the previous chapter. We could try thinking Jesus is reading the passage with us, or to us. As we read (or, better, listen) we need to try to pick up our response. It is often a help to distinguish the simple meaning of the passage (head response) from a felt response (heart response): how does it strike me? What are the echoes? Where do they come from? We generally need to slow down our reading (or listening) to let ourselves tune in to this felt response. And there may be different responses to various words or passages in our reading. We should notice them as best we can, and focus on them later. We may feel it right to stop and pause there to listen more carefully, but if we go on, we should not rush to finish. If we end up doing less than we thought, that is probably for the better.

When we go back to the words that prompted the felt response, we repeat them to ourselves, or find other ways of digesting them. If there were several bits, we must take one of them at a time. As suggested before, we can think of them as food: to be chewed, sucked, and enjoyed. We need to focus on our felt response to them, their 'echo', and let them sink in and nourish us, even if we do not have many thoughts about them. Either way that is where we have begun to pray with them. That is for the next chapter but, even as we pray, we need to keep on listening.

The place of study, reflection and intellectual effort

Something was said in the previous chapter about this. Part of the work of meditation must be to understand the word we are listening to as carefully as possible, and study may make a useful contribution here. Sometimes we will find the scripture we read makes an immediate and inescapable claim on our attention, and that must be a good thing. But it is not always so. Study can help in different ways: we have to pick out God's word from the human language in which the scriptures were written, and their meaning and style sometimes need some work to understand; each genre in the Bible needs a different kind of sensitivity in order to understand its divine intention. Another point is that God's word in a particular passage has to be understood in relation to what he says in the scriptures as a whole. So it is often a real help to mull a particular passage over in conjunction with parallel passages, following up cross-references to other parts of the Old or New Testaments. Early Church Fathers and monks knew the scriptures by heart and were able to do this by recourse to their memories. We can use concordances, marginal references and notes, commentaries a nd dictionaries.

But ultimately the point is always to listen to what the Lord wants to say to us. Perhaps a useful habit to cultivate is to be ready to do a 'quick read' to get the general sense and shape of a passage, or even a whole book of the Bible. A general overview is a help when beginning to focus on a much shorter passage. In working with that, it is useful to take stock fairly quickly of what the passage means from the author's point of view, its 'objective meaning', and then dwell on what it means to me; that is its 'subjective meaning'. Thinking out these two questions separately can help keep the two kinds of meaning separate – not that they are unrelated, but the one can get in the way of the other; and it gives a chance to do the objective work if that is needed. So long as we do not forget that the subjective work is the heart of *lectio divina*, to which we always return, we do not need to suppose that every passage will be full of 'meaning for me' and that *lectio divina* is only about discovering that: there are times, especially when we are reading the Old Testament, when understanding the 'objective meaning' takes far more of our efforts; however, this can promote a personal understanding of other sections of the Bible, and it can help us reach a reflective understanding of ourselves and of God in other ways too. Openness to the spirit, our spirit and God's, is more important than any particular method.

Let the mind play

We read in order to understand, then, and ultimately to understand at a personal level. Part of this work is to understand ourselves before God. This is where the 'felt response' is important as a way of allowing God to touch the thoughts of our hearts, and pray for that purity of heart we have spoken about above. As we read slowly we can give time for our mind to play. We need to be quite free about this. We can let our memory and understanding guide us; this is how our reading enters into and engages with our spirit. This is the heart of the process, which evokes our own experiences of life, our reactions and feelings, our knowledge of ourselves. One way to think about this is to think of *echoes*. If we can listen to the Bible in such a way as to catch echoes of it in our own experience, we are in a good position to begin listening to the word as God's word to us; conversely we can also find our own lives echoing in what we read.

We have to let our minds respond freely to the movement of the spirit. It can seem a little strange to start with, but it helps to remember we are joining in a conversation where we are not always taking the lead. If we are reading slowly we can be sure that the words we have been dwelling on are always there. We can return to them and listen to them again.

Some problems

We can be sure that reading scripture will test us; we will discover we are not good readers; and we are not good listeners. Practice makes perfect! We should never kid ourselves, however, about perfection when we are listening for God and trying to put his word into action. We need to be patient because we are human, and it is enough to be patient with our imperfection, for then God can do his work. Some problems will arise from our own side, however: we may be tired or preoccupied; we may find out how lazy we are as readers, or impatient as listeners. If we are 'achievers' we may have to fight the impulse to want to get on, to 'master' the text, or however we think we can get into a position of control. We may have to face up to our intellectual conccitedness, or our butterfly minds. All this needs a great deal of honesty, patience and good humour. It is all part of the process of learning to listen to God, and to trust in his help and guidance.

There is a deeper problem that we may also find ourselves having to face, a problem of attitude. If we are to become good listeners we need to move from a hermeneutic of suspicion to a hermeneutic of trust. That is to say, we need to accept what we hear and consider what it discloses rather than suppose that we ascertain the truth of what we are reading by discounting or explaining it away. With all the respect due to historians, I think it is more helpful to read the Bible as literature rather than with the distance a historian takes to evidence. Over the last century or so, the tools of historical criticism have opened up a profound understanding of the scriptures; but for us these tools are a help in so far as they help us understand how to read the Bible as literature, and as God's word to us. God's meaning is not to be excavated out of documents; it is to be listened to in faith, hope and love. We must pray God to strengthen these virtues in us; they make us good listeners.

From mind to heart

As the passages for reflection have already indicated, one thing we have to try to do in all this is to get the word out of our heads into our hearts. Some have said that it is the longest journey we ever have to make, and the Orthodox tradition of prayer often talks about prayer as a journey from the mind to the heart. We can find a similar path in *lectio divina*. *Lectio* is a pattern of praying that starts, in the way described in the introduction, by hearing with our ears; then we take the words on our lips as we repeat them to ourselves. The meditation becomes a kind of chewing and digesting! Then as the nutrients we have been given become part of ourselves, they become the stuff of our prayer. But the inner process of digestion takes us right into the centre of our lives, our

69

heart. For that is our living centre, the place where our spirit dwells. That is where God's spirit addresses us, and where we have to learn to listen to him.

It is not easy to find the way to our hearts. We can be very defensive, and the last thing we want to do is to show our defensiveness, and we often prefer not to admit it even to ourselves. Sometimes we have spent a lifetime shoring up the defences, developing various mechanisms to avoid being exposed where it really hurts. But it is from this dehumanizing isolation that our Lord wants to deliver us. If we begin to let God's word touch us, the word will help us find the way to our hearts; it is the key that will unlock the door to the inner room where we are seen by our heavenly Father.

It is not a question of being sentimental about what we read: *lectio divina* is not about cultivating certain kinds of spiritual feeling. Our heart is deeper than our feelings. But the path to our heart is sometimes easier to find if we notice how our feelings are touched by the word of God. Sometimes the word gives us a sense of hope or joy: those kinds of response are fairly straightforward kinds of contact with God. Sometimes our feelings are not so straightforward. Sometimes our lack of feeling, our coldness or apathy, is what we need to reflect on, and let God's word touch. Our heart is reached through the feeling and the lack of it. Then there is the dark side of ourselves. We may be crippled by anger, jealousy, hatred, envy, fear, guilt, despair . . . areas we do not want to look at or be seen, and above all do not want to be touched. But it will be very hard to discover in our spirits a deep relationship of trust and confidence in God on that basis.

And so we should never be embarrassed, startled or afraid when we find ourselves responding to his word in these sorts of ways. That is the forgotten, hurt and damaged part of ourselves that he seeks to heal, bind up and restore. And if we let his word guide us beyond this damage to our capacity to feel and respond to each other as well as to God, we may find that we can eventually let go of that burden, and let God renew our hearts, and, as the psalm says, put a new spirit within us (Psalm 51.10).

The heart is beyond our feelings. If we can find that place where God does touch us with his word, we can also be hopeful that he will heal our sense of hurt or injury; he will enable us to be people of real feeling, and use our emotional energy for good. It may be that we will learn to use our anger in the cause of justice; or that we will be able to love generously, to forgive, all the costly things that can help make the world new.

Spreading meditation over the day

This kind of meditative work is not done quickly. Monks used to spend several hours a day with *lectio divina*! But one possibility to try is to spread *lectio* over a whole day. That is to say, in the morning we can do the reading and have an initial time of prayerful reflection. Later on we can revisit the passage and allow more time for prayer to come out of the more mature reflection that is then possible. Doing it like that gives a chance for the deeper levels of the mind to digest the reading over a longer period and, when we pray, we can engage our heart at once in the fruit of that extended reflection.

Food for the journey

At the start of the chapter, I began by distinguishing the meaning of meditation in *lectio divina* from other kinds of meditation. But before this chapter comes to an end, it is worth pointing out the value of the kind of meditation with a word that is associated with Centering Prayer. Early references to this kind of meditation can be found in John Cassian's discussion of prayer (*Conferences*, *Conf.* 10 on prayer) and in *The Cloud of Unknowing*. For some, especially those whose lives are rather hectic and high-pressured, it may indeed be an extremely useful exercise, especially at the start of a time of meditation with scripture, simply to relax the elaborate defensive systems with which we otherwise face the world, and be ready to allow the word to take us inwards. More generally, it is a good thing to be able to take a word or a phrase away from the time of *lectio divina* and keep returning to it, and repeating it during the day. In this way we can remind ourselves that God is with us through the whole day and we can continue the conversation we started with him when we listened to his word in the scriptures.

New life grows from within, and this process of meditation in *lectio divina* is a source of new life. The disease of the human spirit is its chronic absorption with itself. But prayer is radically different. However far we travel inwards, it is also a reaching out through that inwardness to God and to all things in God. That is the point of transition from meditation to prayer, and to that we must now turn.

Chapter Three:
Praying with the Word

If our meditation with words of scripture teaches us to recognize in them a word of God addressed to us, the most natural thing in the world is for us to reply to it. This response is the movement of prayer, the way we engage in a conversation with God prompted by his word to us. If we have heard the scriptures as a personal address to us, our response must be different from the way we might respond to a book; in that case our reflection will remain something for ourselves. But the scriptures, read in the way of *lectio divina*, draw us into a movement beyond ourselves to God in prayer.

There are, I think, two aspects about our praying that *lectio divina* brings into focus. We learn that prayer is both *response* to a word of God, and that it is a *gift*. As a response to the word of God, prayer is part of a life-long conversation with God. When we respond like this to the scriptures our prayer helps us find God addressing us in every part of our day-to-day lives. But because we often find ourselves responding with the very words of scripture we have received, we are in a position to realize that our praying is given us by God, a gift with which we respond to him. We can come to this realization either because we find ourselves using the word we have received as a simple prayer itself, or because we know how it draws forth and inspires our prayer. At a fundamental level too, the scriptures teach us a language and a grammar with which to pray; they give us the human language God himself uses to speak to us. It is the gift of God, the gift of the Holy Spirit, that we have discovered at work in our hearts through *lectio divina,* that prays in us, drawing our hearts back to God.

Language is the most marvellous avenue of human creativity because it creates relationships between people; it brings people together. It allows me to express myself, and it also allows me to give of myself, to communicate with another. Actually a lot of our language is in practice just making noises, like foghorns sounding off in the night, but when language is properly communicative there can probably be nothing more wonderful or beautiful. Prayer is finding such a relationship with God, and *lectio divina* invites us to let God be our teacher in our praying. As we discover what it is to live in a close relationship with God, we will be able to deepen our relationships with other people. God's way with words helps to purify our resources of language, our capacity for communication and communion.

The way we use language reflects the different ways we relate to people. We all recognize (perhaps with shock) the way going to school changes the language our children use. Where did *that* word come from? In the same way, it is only natural for us who are seeking to keep in touch with God to pick up from his word to us a way of putting things, as well as a way of looking at things, we could learn from no one else. This is not to say that prayer is not us talking from ourselves or that conversation with God has to be stilted, using words with which we do not feel at ease. *Lectio divina* is a way of letting God's word shape us and change us; if prayer arises from reading and meditation, it is precisely a response to a word we have taken to ourselves, a word that has made its home in our hearts, to which we can only say 'Amen'.

One of the deep-rooted problems with our praying is that we have a persistent sense of our unloveliness. We want to hide. We cannot avoid God when we pray; so we avoid prayer. But God does not see us as unlovely, and it can only be a constant source of encouragement to realize in *lectio divina* that God takes the initiative in addressing us because he loves us. In doing so, he gives us the words to teach us to see ourselves differently; he invites us to enter into a conversation with him as between friends. We pray with his word and we discover that it is a word uttered in our heart. It has become *our* word. One of the things he is inviting us to do, as we listen out for his word, is to try to discover and to tune in to the prayer going on secretly in the inner chamber of our hearts. Often it will be in meditating on scripture, in letting it resonate with our spirit, that the word will touch us and lead us to the heart where God, who dwells within, is renewing us in a spirit of prayer.

Praying in response to God's word, then, is a good way to learn that prayer is a relationship with God, and that it is grounded on his love for us. And I think it is good too to pray with words God gives us through our reading of scripture. Not that he needs to be addressed in particular words or a particular style of language. God does not have the ears to hear words in any case; he hears us in our hearts before ever we put anything into words. But we need language to express ourselves, and God uses language for our sakes to help us enter into the relationship that he seeks for us.

Left to ourselves we cannot pray: ancient fathers saw that the fundamental disease of the human spirit is our self-absorption. The word of God heals us by breaking through to our real selves, our hearts, and enabling our lives to be renewed within, from the centre. Prayer is a sign of this renewal of life; it is a gift of the Holy Spirit that God's word releases in our hearts. A sign of our spiritual disease is the loss of our capacity to desire. Of course we easily persuade ourselves there are a thousand things we desire: but they are really only substitutes for real desire; they are just wants, and wants that we easily believe we really need. Our real capacity for desire we have lost because we have lost the sense that we are not made for ourselves, but for God, and that only God satisfies the deepest part of our nature, our desire. He is the joy of our desiring. So the gift of prayer is disclosed above all in the recovery of our desire for God. The prayer that I think is characteristic of *lectio divina* is just this: we delight in his word and want him; we sense our own poverty, weakness or need and want his healing, guidance or strength.

Lectio divina is a big help also in learning to pray for things, either in intercession or in supplication for oneself. This is because God himself teaches us in our reading and meditation the way he sees things; as we learn to see things from his point of view, we learn what he wants, and begin to get a sense of the big picture of his desires and purpose. In this way he is able to teach us to want different things from before, to desire in a different way, according to his will. Our outlook has changed and we begin to adopt his own perspective. *Lectio divina* helps us discover our true orientation towards God, our dependence on his word of love for our very existence.

Desire is the essence of prayer, and, as Augustine remarked, the desire to pray is itself prayer. In the context of *lectio divina* prayer is a chance to realize that desire, to express it. Our reading and meditation on scripture thus helps us discover, in the reaching out of our spirit towards God, that God himself is our teacher. The word, which he utters by his own breath, is a word that gives us breath with which to express our longing. This is a sign that God has begun the long, patient but beautiful work of changing us into the image of his Son.

This chapter is an exploration of how our praying can be shaped in response to patient listening to God's word in *lectio divina*. It is a shorter chapter than the last, because there is much less for us to do, and we have to let God teach us by our own prayer how to respond to him. It begins by reflecting on what Jesus says about prayer in St Matthew's Gospel, together with some similar passages in the other Gospels. These invite us to reflect on the human dimension within which prayer can develop, and above all of the heart as the privileged place of prayer. Then we will turn to the idea of prayer as a gift, as the work of the Spirit in our hearts. As we begin to discover that prayer is not something we do, so much as something we are given, I think it becomes clear how the scriptures open up the encounter between God and ourselves which is central to the dynamic of *lectio divina* and which draws us beyond the text we are reading and meditating with to a loving awareness of God himself, our worship of him and offering ourselves to him.

A Secret Place

Matthew 6.5–6

[5]'And when you pray, you must not be like the hypocrites; for they love to stand and pray in the synagogues and at the street corners, that they may be seen by others. Truly, I say to you, they have received their reward.[6] But when you pray, go into your room and shut the door and pray to your Father who is in secret; and your Father who sees in secret will reward you.'

An ancient understanding of this passage saw the 'inner room' as an image for the heart. We should understand the heart not just as the seat of our feelings, our emotional centre, but deeper than that, as our personal centre. For the earliest monks this was the secret place where we are seen by God, even though he is himself unseen. This is where we find the place of prayer.

The work of listening at this deep level can bring to the light many things that prevent our listening, but with patience we are able to approach our heart. We have already tried to say something about this. Our emotions, in various ways, take us along the path to our heart. The path is a path of prayer, but the place of deep prayer lies beyond them. To enter the inner chamber we have to tune in to our 'felt response' to what we read, and listen carefully to ourselves. It may take some time to get used to, but slowly (and I am putting it very metaphorically) we can learn to find a space between ourselves and the feelings. We *have* the feeling; we are *not the same as* the feeling. This awareness helps us to discern whether our 'felt response' comes from God or from ourselves. More will be said about discernment in the chapter 'Doing the Word'. Then it will be concerned with living the Christian life. But already this process is one that invites prayer from our heart, beyond our feelings, and it purifies our attempts to pray.

This passage is part of a discussion of the three works of righteousness, namely prayer, fasting and almsgiving, in which Jesus contrasts integrity and hypocrisy as a contrast between two ways of life, one where our action is rooted in the depths of our being, our truthfulness towards God, and the other where the motivation for doing things is superficial, to attract attention. Prayer promotes the process of purification, simply by putting us in God's merciful presence and keeping us there. Getting used to not running away, but to being seen by God, promotes the transparency spoken about in the previous chapter (on purity of heart).

We are likely to wake up to our persistent habits of pretence, as well as of self-deception, which Jesus calls 'hypocrisy'. In the context where Jesus is talking he is remarking on our obsession with religious performance. But this obsession goes further than our pride in our image, in 'being seen by others'. It goes as far as how we see ourselves. It all obscures our transparency to God, our ability to let ourselves be seen by him, and to let ourselves reflect his image, in which we have each been created.

Lord Teach Us to Pray

Matthew 6.7–15

[7]'And in praying do not heap up empty phrases as the Gentiles do; for they think that they will be heard for their many words. [8]Do not be like them, for your Father knows what you need before you ask him. [9]Pray then like this: Our Father who art in heaven, hallowed be thy name. [10]Thy kingdom come. Thy will be done, on earth as it is in heaven. [11]Give us this day our daily bread; [12]and forgive us our debts, as we also have forgiven our debtors; [13]and lead us not into temptation, but deliver us from evil. [14]For if you forgive men their trespasses, your heavenly Father also will forgive you; [15]but if you do not

forgive men their trespasses, neither will your Father forgive your trespasses.'

There are two versions of the Lord's Prayer in the Gospels, in Matthew and Luke. Matthew's is the better known as it has been used in the Christian liturgy over the centuries. Both versions occur as part of teaching Jesus gave on how to pray. Matthew includes it together with his teachings on doing things in secret. Luke's rather shorter version (Luke 11.1–4) is given directly in reply to a request by the disciples on how to pray.

In Luke's Gospel, the disciples once asked Jesus to teach them to pray, in the sort of way John the Baptist taught his disciples to pray. It was baffling them that Jesus had not done so, and perhaps it might surprise us that they had to ask, especially as it is clear to us in the Gospels that Jesus was someone who spent a great deal of time in prayer to his Father.

There is no doubt much to learn from such a reaction. Above all, I think, we can learn that for Jesus prayer was such a natural thing, the natural expression of the relationship between himself and his Father, that it did not need to be taught. In a crucial sense, it was not something that can be taught in the way we teach people skills of various kinds. It is not a technique, but a way of being with God, or being towards him. One of the truest lessons in prayer is given in the story of the old man who just sat at the back of the church, who explained: 'I look at God and God looks at me.'

On the other hand, Jesus did teach the disciples how to pray once they had asked, once they had expressed their need and desire to pray; and their going to Jesus to ask for guidance shows that Jesus is central to a person's fully entering into a personal relationship with God. In a similar way Jesus will teach us to pray as we learn to recognize our need and, more than that, our desire to pray. But Christian prayer arises within a relationship like the one between our Lord and his disciples, a relationship where Jesus begins to turn us Godwards. That relationship with God the Father that Jesus makes possible is primary. Prayer is not a technique; it does not produce the relationship, it testifies to it.

That is no doubt why, in Matthew's version, Jesus introduces the Lord's Prayer with a warning against 'heaping up empty phrases'. As with hypocrisy, this kind of performance kills the possibility of a personal relationship with God. Moreover, Jesus teaches us that prayer can only be grounded on the kind of trust that friends have for each other. We do not need to think we have to inform God about things. Prayer testifies to a sense of mutual knowledge, of knowing and being known.

What kind of prayer does that lead to? In the Lord's Prayer we can see a model of the kind of thing Jesus has in mind. Traditionally, commentaries on the Lord's Prayer divide it into two main parts. The first is focused on God, the second on ourselves. This is correct. Prayer arises from a consciousness of God before we open ourselves to him in supplication and contrition.

This is perfectly in accord with what we learn in *lectio divina*. The expression of our own needs must be rooted in the sense of prayer as a response to God. The reality of God is immensely more vital than our awareness of ourselves. Indeed, a real sense of God can open up for us a more realistic sense of ourselves, and of our needs, very different from the one to which we normally pay attention. Above all it can give us the confidence and hope in God's mercy so that we can bring our sinfulness to him for healing and forgiveness, and learn from God's trust in ourselves how to trust others enough to seek to forgive those who are in debt to us. That is what lies behind the way Matthew concludes his commentary on the Lord's Prayer.

Humility in Prayer

The importance of an attitude of repentance for forgiveness is famously the subject of the parable of the Pharisee and the tax collector.

Luke 18.9–14

[9]He also told this parable to some who trusted in themselves that they were righteous and despised others: [10]'Two men went up into the temple to pray, one a Pharisee and the other a tax collector. [11]The Pharisee stood and prayed thus with himself, "God, I thank thee that I am not like other men, extortioners, unjust, adulterers, or even like this tax collector. [12]I fast twice a week, I give tithes of all that I get." [13]But the tax collector, standing far off, would not even lift up his eyes to heaven, but beat his breast, saying, "God, be merciful to me a sinner!" [14]I tell you, this man went down to his house justified rather than the other; for every one who exalts himself will be humbled, but he who humbles himself will be exalted.'

The Pharisee prays 'with himself'; he is too wrapped up in himself to turn *to* anyone. The tax collector stood at a distance, scarcely able to look in God's direction. But he was honest; and, more than that, he did not despair of God's mercy. He it was who went home justified and heard by God.

**   *Lectio divina* teaches us not to be so preoccupied with ourselves, but to start praying in a different place – from our needs rather than our wants, and in the first place our need for God's mercy. It is a place we find by putting ourselves before God, however far off from him we feel ourselves to be. By turning our listening to scripture to prayer we learn to pray more truthfully in this way. We can learn that we have needs and desires we never realized, far deeper than our wants.**

Asking for Things

Prayer is essentially standing before God, acknowledging him as God and ourselves as people in need of his mercy, like the tax collector, but that does not mean we cannot ask for things. There are two passages where Jesus does talk about prayer in this way.

Matthew 7.7–11

[7]'Ask, and it will be given you; seek, and you will find; knock, and it will be opened to you. [8] For every one who asks receives, and he who seeks finds, and to him who knocks it will be opened. [9]Or who among you, if his son asks for bread, will give him a stone? [10]Or if he asks for a fish, will give him a serpent? [11]If you then, who are evil, know how to give good gifts to your children, how much more will your Father who is in heaven give good things to those who ask him!'

Luke 11.5–13

[5]And he said to them, 'Which of you who has a friend will go to him at midnight and say to him, "Friend, lend me three loaves; [6]for a friend of mine has arrived on a journey, and I have nothing to set before him"; [7]and he will answer from within, "Do not bother me; the door is now shut, and my children are with me in bed; I cannot get up and give you anything"? [8]I tell you, though he will not get up and give him anything because he is his friend, yet because of his importunity he will rise and give him whatever he needs. [9]And I tell you, Ask, and it will be given you; seek, and you will find; knock, and it will be opened to you. [10]For everyone who asks receives, and those who seek find, and to the one who knocks it will be opened. [11]What father among you, if his son asks for a fish, will instead of a fish give him a serpent; [12]or if he asks for an egg, will give him a scorpion? [13]If you then, who are evil, know how to give good gifts to your children, how much more will the heavenly Father give the Holy Spirit to those who ask him!'

These two passages are clearly parallel. They illustrate the importance in prayer of two qualities, the need for candour and honesty as well as the need for perseverance. But is there anyone who has not had to live with the challenge to faith of unanswered prayer, of asking and not receiving? As in other instances of Jesus' teaching, Jesus uses paradox to provoke our engagement with God in prayer. For even if we accept cases where we have asked selfishly for things and, in honesty, have not been shocked by not getting them, there are often cases where our requests have not been for stones or scorpions, and we have been denied the bread and fish, either for ourselves or those for whom we have prayed.

So the starting point of a meditation on this passage might be the counter-examples in our own experience of prayer as asking. If so, it will probably recall the anguish as much as the disappointment, the sense of need or compassion out of which we prayed to no avail. Jesus' words, then, challenge us to share our frustration or whatever with him. The chances are we have not faced up to this kind of thing in prayer: most people avoid getting angry with God; but then they bury the grief and pain, and their hearts grow a little colder.

This is not good for us, and it is not good for prayer. This experience is something that anyone who seeks God has to work through, and to work through it with God right there in prayer. But that is the only way we will ever learn, perhaps over a very long time, that God's way is always the way of love and his gifts, even if not the ones we would think of choosing, are good gifts. Only in the struggle of prayer will we learn, above all, the place of suffering and tragedy in the mystery of our redemption, and to begin to say with Jesus his Gethsemane prayer: not my will but thine be done. Only the 'Father who is in heaven' can teach us that we are scarcely beginners in understanding what is truly good, or that 'the things of this world are not worth comparing with the glory of what he has promised'.

Luke's expansion of this teaching develops two themes: the importunate friend illustrates the need for persistence in prayer; and Luke glosses the fact that God gives good gifts in answer to prayer as the gift, above all other gifts, of the Holy Spirit. In the one case, there is a humorous touch in portraying prayer as bothersome, and God as the kind of human being, even a friend, who can get bothered. How much do we take God for granted like that? How attentive are we to him? How much do we let God teach us how different he is from our ways of thinking about him? As far as the other point is concerned, how readily do we take stock of our own desires, taking them so seriously, or the impurity of our hearts? How will we let God teach us how to desire aright? Are we ready to accept what he does want to give us in answer to prayer, or to use the gift of the Holy Spirit to pray after his own mind?

Prayer is a quest for what pleases God ('seek ye first . . .'); God wants to grant us things in answer to our prayer; but we need to learn what his will is. We can do this by listening to his silences. We can begin to learn that the silence that seems to be just an unanswered prayer is the way, or part of the way, God uses to answer our prayer. I will venture a few more remarks on this in the conclusion.

The Gift of Prayer

The last verse of the previous passage from Luke reminds us that true prayer is not something we do from our own resources. The real answer to prayer is the gift of the Holy Spirit, who teaches us to pray aright. In Romans 5.5, Paul tells us that Jesus pours out the Holy Spirit in our hearts and that it is the reassurance of all that we hope for. More importantly the Holy Spirit helps us to pray.

Romans 8.26–27

[26]Likewise the Spirit helps us in our weakness; for we do not know how to pray as we ought, but the Spirit himself intercedes for us with sighs too deep for words. [27]And he who searches human hearts knows what is the mind of the Spirit, because the Spirit intercedes for the saints according to the will of God.

This passage should reassure us. Of course we are weak, of course we will be fearful and uncertain. But the Spirit is at work in our hearts, both to will and to work according to God's good pleasure (Philippians 2.13). If we are open to the Spirit in our *lectio divina*, and act sincerely in faith, hope and love, we must believe that God will be with us. The Spirit prays for us and gives us help. In a real sense we can leave it to him.

The Holy Spirit is himself the spirit of prayer, which searches the mind of God: it helps us understand how God is continually giving us his gifts – and to ask for things which God wants to give us. The Spirit guides us to seek his will in our prayer, and to be ready to say 'Not my will but thine be done'.

To discover prayer in our hearts as a gift of the Spirit is already to have begun to discover the joy of *lectio divina* in contemplation. It is to wake up to the fact that prayer unites us to God, and that in the Holy Spirit we share in the life of the Trinity. This is something we will look at in the final chapter, 'Living by the Word'.

Two Ways of Prayer

To conclude our reflections on what the Gospels teach us about the place of prayer as a response to God's word, we ought to consider the story of Martha and Mary.

Luke 10.38–42

[38]Now as they went on their way, he entered a village; and a woman named Martha received him into her house. [39]And she had a sister called Mary, who sat at the Lord's feet and listened to his teaching. [40]But Martha was distracted with much serving; and she went to him and said, 'Lord, do you not care that my sister has left me to serve alone? Tell her then to help me.' [41]But the Lord answered her, 'Martha, Martha, you are anxious and troubled about many things; [42]one thing is needful. Mary has chosen the good portion, which shall not be taken away from her.'

Over the centuries, the story of the two sisters has been considered from many points of view. Each of them exemplifies a way of praying. Martha, active and busy, prays with an urgent, albeit selfish request. Mary just sits at the Lord's feet and listens to Jesus talking. Just as there should be a place for both sisters in our lives, an active life as well as the quieter, more reflective life, devoted simply to God, so there is scope both for asking for things in prayer as well as just listening at the Lord's feet. In a way, Jesus prefers Mary's prayer to Martha's, but only because our prayer so often expresses more our worries and fretfulness than our loving attention to God himself. But, in practice, it is perhaps only by praying from our distractedness that we can let Jesus gently draw us to listening more patiently and praying more simply. Both sisters have something to teach us: by sitting with Mary and learning from Jesus we will be able to serve our Lord as faithfully as Martha did. This takes us into the final phase of *lectio divina*, contemplation, and, beyond that, to how we put the word into practice.

Practical Section

The whole point of *lectio divina* is to find God speaking to us in the scriptures. The essential thing is to learn to listen and to respond.

Prayer is the way in which we do listen and begin to respond. In a sense I do not think much more can be said about how to pray, so long as we have begun to listen and are honest and courageous in our response.

As I have tried to explain in the main part of the chapter, we may well be prompted by our reading and meditation to ask for things, and we should not be afraid to do so, or to try to put our response to God's word into words of our own. I do think that candour is something we need in our prayer: someone I know said he first really prayed when he told God how boring he was! God never bored him again!

It is good to open up a conversation with God, and let his word build up a confident and trustful relationship with him. It also helps to draw the word more deeply into our hearts, and bring us to a deeper knowledge of ourselves as people addressed by God, a Father who loves us. So, however inept our requests, if we listen to the Spirit in our hearts as we ponder on God's word, we will grow in our prayer because we will let the Spirit pray in us. It is the only way we will learn how to pray according to the mind of Christ.

One thing must be said. We must be ready to stop reading whenever we find ourselves turning to God, and be ready to carry on in due course. Stopping can be a difficulty if we are addicted to reading. This is really something that we have mentioned under meditation. Perhaps the thing we have to take care with is to remember that our reading is really listening, one side of a conversation that we ought to join in. Our reading should be more than making us think; we are trying to listen to God, and we need not be shy to turn to him.

In the main part of this chapter we have said something about *lectio* and *meditatio* helping us find the place of prayer in our hearts. Prayer is a matter of entering into that place, finding ourselves in God's presence, and not being in a hurry to get away. Once there, we can put things into words or just be there quietly. We can remember that the Holy Spirit, which has helped us tune in to God's word, is praying in us, with us and for us. That is the gift of prayer.

Perhaps something more should be said about silence. If we learn to listen in prayer, we will find that we spend a lot of time listening to silence. Ignatius of Antioch said that God speaks by silence. He does so because that is the kind of space needed for our hearts to be touched by him and to be changed. Communication between human beings takes place linguistically because that is the way we relate to each other as human beings in the material world. When we think how we are related to God, it is not one to one in the same way. He is our creator, and we exist because he calls us continually into being. That is not a linguistic, but an existential relationship. I think he joins in and responds to our prayer by the way we find in him our life and being. The silence that helps deepen our awareness of that interiority and dependence on him, in which we are increasingly open to his grace, is a silence that speaks more eloquently than any words. On the other hand we are linguistic creatures, and it is right for us to use language to address ourselves to him when we need to, and he has given us his word in the Bible to prompt our response to him in prayer. But in the end, the only thing that matters is our faith, our hope, and our love.

If we are reading in the meditative way we have described, listening out for God's word, we may find that we just are praying rather than reading. If we are unfamiliar with this, we may find it a rather strange state; it will be hard to tell the difference between our prayerful reading and our prayerful response to our reading. That does not matter. Neither does it matter if our prayer seems hardly to form itself into words or clear ideas: the Spirit searches the heart and, in any case, we do not know how to pray as we ought. Just remember that God is close to us and between close friends a great deal can be left unsaid. Perhaps the best prayer will be just wanting God. It will help put all our other wanting in perspective – and wake us up to our real neediness.

At the end of the time of *lectio divina* it is very good to make a prayer of thanksgiving, and make more specific prayers for people or needs of our own that have come into our time of *lectio*, and especially that we may live the rest of the day in the light of God's word.

A final thought: prayer goes hand in hand with our listening and reading; it helps us to receive the words more deeply. *Lectio* does not move in straight lines from one kind of operation to the next; it spirals around these various elements, both upwards and downwards. Downwards it takes us more deeply into ourselves, into our hearts, what scripture calls the secret place. Upwards it draws us more and more into an awareness of God, the process that is perhaps better left to the next chapter when we consider contemplation as part of a process of wondering.

Chapter Four:
Wondering at the Word

Prayer, in the sense we were thinking about in the previous chapter, is only the start of our response to God. An important part of our response is to do something, to put the word into practice. That is the subject of the chapter that follows. In this chapter, I want to consider a further movement of prayer traditionally associated with *lectio divina*, where the heart turns in love and worship, or in whatever way the scripture has spoken to our hearts, from the words of prayer to God himself, so that we simply stay in his presence and let him be. If scripture prompts us to turn to God in prayer, we should not be surprised that God is more absorbing than anything he has to say to us in our reading, or we to him. This movement of adoration and self-surrender, with or without words, is the final movement of the traditional fourfold process of *lectio divina*.

In the Middle Ages this final stage was called contemplation, but I think this term nowadays either says too little to people, or it says far too much! It became a very loaded term and was used to refer to the highest and most extraordinary flights of mystical exaltation. Conversely, nowadays the term 'contemplative prayer' is often used to mean any state of deep, silent prayer (confusingly also called 'meditative prayer'); it refers to a kind of psychological state without necessarily any idea that it is a response to God. This chapter is not an introduction to contemplation in either of these senses of the word. Books on mystical prayer will deal with that. But there are links, and I am sure that the writers of the Christian mystical tradition would have taken for granted that this kind of prayer is only the blossoming of our response to God who addresses us in the scriptures and who invites us to enter more deeply into the mystery of faith revealed and culminating in Jesus Christ.

In fact what needs to be said here is a bit simpler and more down to earth. It is the most obvious thing in the world to listen to the speaker rather than the words, to realize that our attention is directed towards him and rests in him. Once we begin to hear the word of God and incline our hearts to it, we are ultimately attending to him rather than to it. If we let it touch us, we are invited to wake up to the fact that we are being affected by more than just words. In dwelling on what God says to us and in praying with it, we begin to realize how closely God enters into our lives, and how intimately our lives are wrapped up in his. We are able to discover in prayer our desire for God, our need of his love and mercy; and as his word finds an echo in our hearts, our spirit resonates with the Spirit that God pours out on us in our hearts. What is called contemplation is simply our discovery and thankful appreciation of the fact that we have found him whom our souls seek; we have found our hearts' desire.

In trying to engage with this final moment of prayerful response to God's word, I want to consider things from a slightly different angle, because I think that in practice our praying with scripture does lead us on from the text to something rather bigger, but it is not always something we feel can be dignified with a term anything so illustrious as 'contemplation'. It can be felt as a more problematic and uncertain state. Instead, I want to use the term 'wondering'. Wonder can cover a range of responses. It can, of course, mean the sense of admiration, even the sense of being taken out of oneself, that is analogous to the religious sense of heightened awareness traditionally referred to by 'contemplation'. It is our natural response to beauty and, beyond that, it is an attitude that summons and expresses our love. So it is not just a passive state, it calls forth our gift of ourselves. But it can mean a more perplexed state of mind: 'I wonder what . . . , if . . . ,' and so on. Wonder can represent a state of understanding: at the conclusion of a search for the answer to a problem, I can wonder at the beauty of the solution, or at my own stupidity in not seeing it before; it can be like sitting back to enjoy the finished crossword puzzle. Or wonder can be the recognition of the way my experience of something exceeds my capacity to understand it. Wonder can be part of the search or the conclusion of it, it can be a joyful state or something much harder to come to terms with. To use a distinction drawn by Ruth Burrows in a different context (in her *Guidelines for Mystical Prayer*), it can be 'lights on' or 'lights off'.

Common to all these kinds of wonder, I think, is that they demand receptivity and surrender rather than analysis and thought. Understanding here is more a case of seeing than of thinking – although there may well be implications to think about. But the moment of wonder itself is a moment of insight or discovery, or a critical phase on the path to it. The important thing is the need to be open, a readiness to be changed by the experience. This openness allows the deeper resources of the self, the dimension of the spirit, to come into action. Wonder opens us up to the discovery of God.

Such is the world we live in that I think our capacity for wonder has often not been given a proper chance to develop, and our lives of faith are much the poorer as a result. Moreover, we do not like the dark, and the darker kinds of wondering, our perplexity with God, our sense of having lost our way, are states of mind we need time to learn to see as important parts of our journey. We journey by faith not sight. *Lectio divina* can be a help here. With its light and dark places, the world of the scriptures teaches us to see our own world, with its highs and lows, as a world that invites us to make a similar journey of faith to that we read in the Bible. It can only encourage us that we read there how God continues to call all things to find their fulfilment in him, in spite of prevarication and sin, and even though people never saw that hope fulfilled in their lives. Hebrews 11 is an example of one author's reading of the story in those terms.

Lectio divina therefore helps educate our perception of life, to see the place in it of the different seasons of the spirit, times of wintering and loss as well as those of new life and fruitfulness. It helps us find our proper orientation towards God, what I like to call our 'godwardness'. This is how I think the darker kinds of wondering can be understood. They are the places where patience is needed, places of waiting for a resolution we can never provide for ourselves, but which will be given. They may be times when our faith, hope and love are tried sorely, when we feel we have no more strength of our own, but have to learn to receive what only God can give. The word 'godwardness' is one that for me points to a direction even though we cannot actually make out what we are looking for. If you want to see the kingfisher, all you can do is go down to where he has been seen and at the times he is likely to be there. Ultimately we do not wait in vain.

Waking up to our godwardness allows us to discover wondering as an ultimately positive thing. Whether it is a 'lights on' or a 'lights off' experience, it puts us in the way of acquiring a state of mind that enables us to find God in all things, and to find all things in God; and finally it helps us find ourselves in God's image.

We find God in all things as the scriptures teach us to pick out the dialogue between God's grand design to save mankind and the sort of very un-grand but human ways in which people's need for him is felt. We learn how God works in history and in the texture of human lives, calling people to himself. They help us connect more hopefully (and therefore positively) with our anxiety, or our anger, at the apparent absence of God from situations of human crisis and need. For they show that God is never absent from our suffering. *Lectio divina* teaches us to find God in the very mundane circumstances of our world, and how our own relationship to him must develop in very concrete terms. This is what faith is all about, and for which the Bible's story of faith is our constant guide.

But finding God in all things is only the flip side to finding all things in God, and realizing that he is the ultimate reality by whom, through whom and in whom we share existence. We are not the centre of the story. This we learn from finding that we have been made in the image of

God. We only reflect glory; the wonder of life and human achievement is a gift from God, and it carries with it a responsibility to serve. This is a knowledge we come to best of all in *lectio divina*, as we let the word bring us to ourselves, disclose our real need for God, and create in us a new heart with which to desire him who alone satisfies it.

So wondering helps us to find the centre outside ourselves, in relation to others and to God. This process of de-centring is vitally important for our spiritual maturity. But it is a terribly demanding process, going against the current of so much in secular culture. It is bound to leave us wondering, and we must expect it to have important repercussions on our outlook and on our most ordinary commitments. It must change our lives. That is the link with the last chapter of this book, 'Living by the Word'.

In the passages that follow it is worth exploring various ways in which wondering is treated in the New Testament. Perhaps we will be able to identify with some of them. Briefly, we will look at the way people responded to Jesus' teaching, and to his miracles of healing. We should notice how the experience of wonder was not always a response of welcome, or of faith. It provoked opposition and condemnation too. Some of the stories suggest how wonder connects with related emotions, such as curiosity and fear, and how these can become paths to faith. Finally we need to remember that the mystery of the cross and the Lord's resurrection, the greatest miracle of all, teach us that wonder is in some way fundamental to Christian faith, and a precondition of worship.

The Sense of Wonder

The most obvious account of wonder is what people felt in response to Jesus' teaching. We have already noted the sense of authority people felt. This felt response, the sense of 'impact', was important: it opened them up to an experience of God, beyond the actual words of his teaching, which Jesus wanted them to discover. The exhilaration, the liberation of hope people felt was itself an experience of the Kingdom that he had come to inaugurate. Even if the response was expressed as a question, 'What is this new teaching?', it was already a response of faith, as yet undeclared, but born of the hope that they felt Jesus addressed. It is something that we should take time to notice as we listen to his teaching ourselves.

This is how Jesus talked about this kind of response; he was picking up the disciples' question about his parables:

Matthew 13.10–11, 16–17

[10]Then the disciples came and said to him, 'Why do you speak to them in parables?' [11]And he answered them, 'To you it has been given to know the secrets of the kingdom of heaven, but to them it has not been given. . . . [16]But blessed are your eyes, for they see, and your ears, for they hear. [17]Truly, I say to you, many prophets and righteous people longed to see what you see, and did not see it, and to hear what you hear, and did not hear it.'

Wonder is prompted by our understanding of God's meaning in the story of Jesus and the whole story of salvation which hinges on him, from the very first adumbrations of it as promised in the Old Testament to the way God is working out our salvation within the story of the last times. It is built on a sense of hope, which our reading of scripture should nurture.

It is not always easy to see the picture very clearly in our own life and times. So often we find ourselves living in a twilight zone. But if we can learn to wonder at the good news in the Gospels, for instance, and notice how God works over the longer time-spans of the Old Testament, we can find points of insight into the present time as well.

These moments Jesus calls moments of blessing. They are moments when we realize God is smiling on us. Cultivating a

sense of that smile, be it one of sympathy or of encouragement, opens up the path of new life as a blessing to others.

Matthew 11.25–27

[25]At that time Jesus declared, 'I thank you, Father, Lord of heaven and earth, that you have hidden these things from the wise and understanding and revealed them to babes; [26]yes, Father, for such was your gracious will. [27]All things have been delivered to me by my Father; and no one knows the Son except the Father, and no one knows the Father except the Son and any one to whom the Son chooses to reveal him.'

The natural response to a blessing is to bless, which means the same as to give thanks. Jesus' sense of God's blessing is expressed in his own readiness to bless. We too will find our outlook is transformed as we learn to give thanks for everything; for this reflects our growing appreciation of how everything is a gift from a generous Father.

At one level this short passage reminds us that one of the reasons for practising *lectio divina* is to learn to find our lives within the horizons of the great work of salvation achieved by Christ in establishing his Kingdom. Then we can give thanks where it is due. More than that, our lives become part of the mystery of the Kingdom, which is hidden from the wise and clever, but revealed to the simple, who have come to know Jesus as the Son of God.

We can compare this blessing with that given to Peter.

Matthew 16.17

[17]And Jesus answered him, 'Blessed are you, Simon Bar-Jona! For flesh and blood has not revealed this to you, but my Father who is in heaven.'

Always this level of understanding is a gift of God, a precious, often unexpected moment, when we suddenly see something from God's point of view. Here the moment is Peter's recognition of Christ. He was able to move beyond knowledge of the scriptures and the history of God's work of salvation to understand what God was doing in the present.

It was a moment of radical understanding, and the implications of it took him a long time to appreciate: Jesus' next words to him were 'Get behind me Satan. You are a stumbling block to me; for you are on the side of human beings, not of God!' Peter thought he could take advantage of his insight. It is a significant moment for us; always in *lectio divina* the moment of discovery will be a moment where we discover the presence of Jesus in our lives. And the next moment will be one where we have to let him work his own work, through us or for us, on his own terms.

But, as with Peter, the moment of discovery contains a summons to discipleship: 'Anyone who would come after me must take up his cross (even daily) and follow me.'

The Marvel of Life Made Whole

Healing also prompted wonder. If we let God touch us with his word, we will be changed by it, and perhaps the most striking cause of our wonder is like that of people in the Gospels wondering at Jesus' ministry of healing. We should notice the different circumstances that bring people to Jesus, sometimes desperation, sometimes hope. The miracles of healing are a demonstration of power and compel attention to the person of our Lord. But they are not just a demonstration of power; the Gospels repeatedly present healing as a response to faith. Sometimes the faith is fully fledged, sometimes it is much less confident: 'Lord, I believe; help my unbelief' was the cry of the father of the epileptic demoniac after the Transfiguration (Mark 9.24). Here, as elsewhere, it was the faith of the people who brought the sick to Jesus that counts.

Their response to his teaching was complex; wonder sometimes called forth faith, but sometimes a question about where he got his power. In Nazareth, where people thought they knew all there was to know about Jesus, he could do very few works of healing: he was amazed at their lack of faith (Mark 6.6; compare the parallel in Matthew 13.58 below). In our *lectio divina* we will perhaps find ourselves struggling with the implications of a similar move to a position of faith.

More generally, the scriptures describe many different cases of people searching for God or for Jesus out of a sense of need. Nietzsche complained that Christianity was a religion for losers. But in fact the people who searched found! The real point is that what was missing, these people's real source of need, was a relationship with God, the God of compassion and mercy, who meets us in all our suffering. We live not as individuals in isolation from each other, but as people shaped by relationships with each other, and especially by that relationship which is central to our existence as human beings, with God, our Father and creator, our Saviour and the source of new life in the Spirit. It is the recognition and appreciation of that relationship that above all promotes wholeness of life.

Matthew 15.29–31

[29]And Jesus went on from there and passed along the Sea of Galilee. And he went up on the mountain, and sat down there. [30]And great crowds came to him, bringing with them the lame, the maimed, the blind, the dumb, and many others, and they put them at his feet, and he healed them, [31]so that the throng wondered, when they saw the dumb speaking, the maimed whole, the lame walking, and the blind seeing; and they glorified the God of Israel.

The passage is the preamble to Matthew's account of the Feeding of the Four Thousand, a miracle of feeding that reminds us of the

Janice Smyth, Martin Bradley and Janet Davies.

...dentists officials and dental health professionals Oral Cancer includes cancer of the lip, mouth and pharynx. It is a significant disease in Northern Ireland. Figures from the Northern Ireland Cancer Registry show that in 2006 there were a total of 183 cases of oral cancers diagnosed, of which 123 were men and 60 were women. It also showed that the five-year survival rate for oral cancer is on average less than 50 per cent.

The event was addressed by the acting said dentists can play a valuable role in identifying the disease.

"I have personal experience of this when I found oral cancer affecting a very fit, non smoking, non drinking, ex-county and provincial hurler, single figure handicap golfer and great friend. Thankfully, he survived because of early detection and intervention. It is not incurable, but people need to be aware that early detection is a key to survival. I would encourage everyone to get regular dental checkups as highly publicised such as cervical cancer."

Key signs that should be looked for include: mouth ulcers that don't heal, white or red patches in the mouth and any unusual changes in the mouth. Currently the best chance of biting back against oral cancer comes from early detection

■ Visit your dentist
■ Adopt a healthy diet and lifestyle
■ Stop smoking

Common complaints answered

THE ALTERNATIVE

Caroline Bickerstaff
Dip. CNM MBANT
Cert. ECBS

Holistic and
Nutritional Therapist
The Natural Health Clinic
796 695379

awful. Is there anything I can do to keep these at bay?

A. Cold sores are a classic sign that the immune system is under pressure. This virus only gets a grip when your immune system is compromised, usually by a poor diet and lifestyle with a lot of stress. In my experience of working with these, getting more raw foods into the diet certainly helps; fruit on a daily basis and salads gives your body the means to build a stronger immunity. Chocolate, alcohol and coffee don't help the situation so start cutting back on these.

Boost your immune system by taking direct on the area where you feel the tingling – keep applying on an hourly basis.

Q. Dear Caroline, my hayfever is back again this year with a vengeance and I hate taking anti-histamines continuously but if I don't, my eyes and nose stream constantly, making it almost impossible to go outside. What can I do?

A. Cut out wheat, dairy, soya and red meat as these foods are mucous forming, exacerbating the problem. Avoid alcohol and coffee too. Wheat...

Eucharist, and of our deepest need for nourishment by God. But the reference at the end of the excerpt recalls the prophecy of Isaiah, for example Isaiah 35.5–6, where the prophet looks ahead to the Messianic times. In Matthew 11.2–5, these are the signs that Jesus says should be an encouragement to John the Baptist, that the one he foretold has indeed come.

So once again the Gospel writer implies that the sense of wonder people felt at the miracles was an appreciation of Jesus, albeit implicit and not yet an articulate faith, as the one who inaugurates the Kingdom of God.

Nor should we be afraid to approach God with our needs. Rather we should be encouraged to respond to our sense of need by searching for Jesus in the scriptures and presenting ourselves to him so that we may be healed. That experience of healing will help us celebrate the Eucharist with deeper and more heartfelt praise, where Jesus will feed us spiritually so that we may do his will.

Among the many particular stories of healing in the Gospels is that of the paralytic, who is so helpless that his cure depends on the ingenuity of those who carried him to Jesus.

Mark 2.1–12

[1]And when he returned to Capernaum after some days, it was reported that he was at home. [2]And many were gathered together, so that there was no longer room for them, not even about the door; and he was preaching the word to them. [3]And they came, bringing to him a paralytic carried by four men. [4]And when they could not get near him because of the crowd, they removed the roof above him; and when they had made an opening, they let down the pallet on which the paralytic lay. [5]And when Jesus saw their faith, he said to the paralytic, 'My son, your sins are forgiven.' [6]Now some of the scribes were sitting there, questioning in their hearts, [7]'Why does

this man speak thus? It is blasphemy! Who can forgive sins but God alone?' [8]And immediately Jesus, perceiving in his spirit that they thus questioned within themselves, said to them, 'Why do you question thus in your hearts? [9]Which is easier, to say to the paralytic, "Your sins are forgiven," or to say, "Rise, take up your pallet and walk"? [10]But that you may know that the Son of man has authority on earth to forgive sins' – he said to the paralytic – [11]'I say to you, rise, take up your pallet and go home.' [12]And he rose, and immediately took up the pallet and went out before them all; so that they were all amazed and glorified God, saying, 'We never saw anything like this!'

In the early Church this parable was given an allegorical interpretation: the house is ourselves and to find healing we need to move from a life focused on externals and undertake a journey inwards, to our hearts. That is where Jesus is to be found.

The fact that we cannot get down there on our own, but have to be lowered, teaches us that we depend on others in the family of faith: in fact it is their faith that Jesus seems to be commending when he heals the paralytic, so helpless is he.

And there is the other point that sin paralyses our lives in so many ways. The word of healing we need is actually a simple word of forgiveness.

In the context of *lectio divina* the story also highlights, in the figure of Jesus' teaching, how it is by getting into our hearts and listening to Jesus speaking as we meditate on the scriptures that we can find a word of release, a word of healing and a word of forgiveness. Perhaps we do not even appreciate our sinfulness until we discover we can begin to live in the new way Jesus makes possible for us.

But there is also the hubbub of discussion in the house as the miracle takes place. The arguments, the questions and scepticism may well be in our own hearts together with the desperate effort of faith to reach Jesus. The only proof, the only way to deal with the questions and the doubt, is to get up and walk. And to praise God.

The story reminds us that wonder is not just a 'wow' or a 'whoopee': it can be doubtful, questioning, even fearful. Revelation is not always welcome: sometimes it provokes hostility; and it always demands a change of heart.

The ambiguities in people's response to moments of revelation are well shown in the Gospels.

Matthew 13.53–58

[53] And when Jesus had finished these parables, he went away from there, [54] and coming to his own country he taught them in their synagogue, so that they were astonished, and said, 'Where did this man get this wisdom and these mighty works? [55] Is not this the carpenter's son? Is not his mother called Mary? And are not his brothers James and Joseph and Simon and Judas? [56] And are not all his sisters with us? Where then did this man get all this?' [57] And they took offence at him. But Jesus said to them, 'A prophet is not without honour except in his own country and in his own house.' [58] And he did not do many mighty works there, because of their unbelief.

The crowds' amazement in Nazareth is similar to that felt at Capernaum (Mark 1.27). But the response here is sceptical to the point of rejection rather than one of hope and admiration. The story can be turned round to help us examine our own prejudices in listening to scripture: do we welcome it, or are we sceptical? Do we read with a 'hermeneutic of suspicion' or of hope? What does it take to shift from one to the other? I think people's faith generally rubs shoulders with unbelief, and the questions in our minds could seem to take us either way. The

decisive thing is that if we have known Jesus, if we have come
to believe in him and have shared some sense of the hope he
inspires, these are experiences that are extremely hard to jet-
tison, even if we do not really feel that this *is* faith. But that
feeling is a mistake.

Positive and Negative Poles of Wonder

Another story that brings these two attitudes to Jesus together is the one
of the woman who came into the Pharisee's house and anointed his feet
with perfume. The woman's response of adoration provokes puzzlement, if not scandal. The contrast suggests the kind of difficulty that the
invitation to faith in Jesus can pose.

Luke 7.36–50

[36]One of the Pharisees asked him to eat with him, and he went into
the Pharisee's house, and took his place at table. [37]And behold, a
woman of the city, who was a sinner, when she learned that he was
at table in the Pharisee's house, brought an alabaster flask of ointment, [38]and standing behind him at his feet, weeping, she began to
wet his feet with her tears, and wiped them with the hair of her
head, and kissed his feet, and anointed them with the ointment.
[39]Now when the Pharisee who had invited him saw it, he said to
himself, 'If this man were a prophet, he would have known who and
what sort of woman this is who is touching him, for she is a sinner.'
[40]And Jesus answering said to him, 'Simon, I have something to say to
you.' And he answered, 'What is it, Teacher?' [41]'A certain creditor
had two debtors; one owed five hundred denarii, and the other fifty.
[42]When they could not pay, he forgave them both. Now which of
them will love him more?' [43]Simon answered, 'The one, I suppose,
to whom he forgave more.' And he said to him, 'You have judged
rightly.' [44]Then turning toward the woman he said to Simon, 'Do you
see this woman? I entered your house, you gave me no water for

my feet, but she has wet my feet with her tears and wiped them with her hair. [45]You gave me no kiss, but from the time I came in she has not ceased to kiss my feet. [46]You did not anoint my head with oil, but she has anointed my feet with ointment. [47]Therefore I tell you, her sins, which are many, are forgiven, for she loved much; but he who is forgiven little, loves little.' [48]And he said to her, 'Your sins are forgiven.' [49]Then those who were at table with him began to say among themselves, 'Who is this, who even forgives sins?' [50]And he said to the woman, 'Your faith has saved you; go in peace.'

This is a different kind of story, and it is worth trying to read it as a drama between two parts of ourselves, between the recklessness of love and a more rational way of thinking.

It shows, on the one hand, the extravagance of the woman's intimacy with Jesus, which can be prompted by prayer. This is spontaneous, personal and regardless of anything else, concerned only to respond to Jesus' love and his loveableness. On the other hand the reaction of the socially aware Pharisee, judicious, constantly judging things by moral standards, seems unable to connect with Jesus in any real way. As in the previous excerpt, the story dramatizes two styles of interpreting Jesus. Both bring people into contact with Jesus; only one is an experience of salvation. And that is because the woman knows her need for Jesus and does not count the cost.

Rather as with the cure of the paralytic (Mark 2.1–12) Jesus shows his divinity by forgiveness of sins. Here the story does not focus on conflict with the authorities; it focuses simply on the woman herself. Her experience of Jesus' love prompts her lavish demonstration of affection. Jesus does not actually say that it is because he had previously forgiven her; his words imply that her extraordinary and scandalous gesture has won her forgiveness.

Wonder as a Rejection of Faith

But wonder can mean rejection. It is a sad moment when, after Jesus had fed the five thousand and, in John's account, had talked about himself as the Bread of Life, many of those who had followed him began to turn away; Jesus had gone too far (John 6.66–69). Peter then speaks up for the rest and says there is no one else to whom they can turn: Jesus has the word of eternal life. It is our ability to hold on to that kind of certainty, and the hope it expresses, that enables faith to grow beyond our capacity at first to understand, and to meet the challenge that Jesus' teaching will always make.

Other people, though, approach Jesus with their minds made up, interested really in trying to catch him out. At the end of the Gospel story, after Jesus enters Jerusalem on Palm Sunday, the Gospel writers tell an increasingly conflictual story. Jesus provokes all the main groups of the Jewish establishment who unite and denounce him to Pilate. Here is a case where people marvel at Jesus without faith; the experience only provokes increased hostility. The scene is the debate over whether the Jews should pay taxes to the Roman state.

Matthew 22.21b–22

[21] Jesus said to them, 'Render therefore to Caesar the things that are Caesar's, and to God the things that are God's.' [22] When they heard it, they marvelled; and they left him and went away.

The detail of wonder, 'marvelling', picked out here by Matthew is equivalent to hostility and a sign of a lack of faith. As an illustration of *lectio divina* it reminds us that faith is an essential condition for discovering God in Jesus. The scriptures in fact provide a source of judgement of our faith. For those who read without faith the experience will be one that provokes anger or scepticism. Those who read with faith will find joy and hope, as well as a challenge to discipleship.

Similarly, at the start of the Gospel, the cures that create the sense of wonder we have already noted also provoke hostility. The moves some people made to destroy Jesus started early in the ministry, with the curing of a man on the Sabbath (Mark 3.6).

Wonder as Curiosity

Zacchaeus gives an example of a different kind of wonder: here we see the power of curiosity at the start of the journey of faith, drawing someone to want to see Jesus, even if intending to keep safely out of the way! It does not stop Jesus' spotting him and inviting himself to visit, a visit that changes Zacchaeus' life. As with the sinful woman it releases enormous generosity – here towards other people.

Luke 19.1–10

[1]He entered Jericho and was passing through. [2]And there was a man named Zacchaeus; he was a chief tax collector, and rich. [3]And he sought to see who Jesus was, but could not, on account of the crowd, because he was small of stature. [4]So he ran on ahead and climbed up into a sycamore tree to see him, for he was to pass that way. [5]And when Jesus came to the place, he looked up and said to him, 'Zacchaeus, make haste and come down; for I must stay at your house today.' [6]So he made haste and came down, and received him joyfully. [7]And when they saw it they all murmured, 'He has gone in to be the guest of a man who is a sinner.' [8]And Zacchaeus stood and said to the Lord, 'Behold, Lord, the half of my goods I give to the poor; and if I have defrauded any one of anything, I restore it fourfold.' [9]And Jesus said to him, 'Today salvation has come to this house, since he also is a son of Abraham. [10]For the Son of man came to seek and to save the lost.'

Perhaps this story reminds us that we must not be surprised to find *lectio divina* having a revolutionary impact on our lives. If we go out to look for Jesus it is hard to keep a safe distance.

The heart of the story is telling. In *lectio divina* we need to try to find Jesus and look at him. But we can also find that Jesus is looking at us. We need to give time in our *lectio divina* for that exchange of looks. It can change our lives.

Wonder and Fear

The sea seems to have been a place of revelation of Jesus' power in several stories. The disciples were fishermen and experienced on the water. It is encouraging to know that not even they were immune to fear in a storm.

Mark 4.35–41

[35]On that day, when evening had come, he said to them, 'Let us go across to the other side.' [36]And leaving the crowd, they took him with them in the boat, just as he was. And other boats were with him. [37]And a great storm of wind arose, and the waves beat into the boat, so that the boat was already filling. [38]But he was in the stern, asleep on the cushion; and they woke him and said to him, 'Teacher, do you not care if we perish?' [39]And he awoke and rebuked the wind, and said to the sea, 'Peace! Be still!' And the wind ceased, and there was a great calm. [40]He said to them, 'Why are you afraid? Have you no faith?' [41]And they were filled with awe, and said to one another, 'Who then is this, that even wind and sea obey him?'

In contrast to the way Romantics found the transcendent in wild landscapes and violent phenomena, God is not revealed here in the storm; the storm is only destructive, a symbol of chaos before creation. God's power is revealed in the obedience of the winds and waves to his command. Characteristically too the experience of Jesus' divinity springs from the panic of despair. 'Master! Do you not care?'

When the storm was settled, their question 'Who then is this?' is at the same time a cry of shock and of recognition of divine power. The emotion of fear seems to go through several changes in this passage, emerging as wonder as well as hesitation at the power they experience. Jesus tells his disciples after the Resurrection not to be afraid; but it is a natural emotion, which we need to accept honestly before we can find it changed into wonder and even the confidence of faith.

This story of Jesus walking on the water takes things further:

Matthew 14.22–33

[22]Then he made the disciples get into the boat and go before him to the other side, while he dismissed the crowds. [23]And after he had dismissed the crowds, he went up on the mountain by himself to pray. When evening came, he was there alone, [24]but the boat by this time was many furlongs distant from the land, beaten by the waves; for the wind was against them. [25]And in the fourth watch of the night he came to them, walking on the sea. [26]But when the disciples saw him walking on the sea, they were terrified, saying, 'It is a ghost!' And they cried out for fear. [27]But immediately he spoke to them, saying, 'Take heart, it is I; have no fear.' [28]And Peter answered him, 'Lord, if it is you, bid me come to you on the water.' [29]He said, 'Come.' So Peter got out of the boat and walked on the water and came to Jesus; [30]but when he saw the wind, he was afraid, and beginning to sink he cried out, 'Lord, save me.' [31]Jesus immediately reached out his hand and caught him, saying to him, 'O man of little faith, why did you doubt?' [32]And when they got into the boat, the wind ceased. [33]And those in the boat worshipped him, saying, 'Truly you are the Son of God.'

Again we can derive confidence from knowing that Jesus comes to us in the midst of a storm. Perhaps we can find even more help from the detail that Jesus, in his night prayer, is with his disciples and knows that they are in distress.

The main point of this story is not so much that Jesus calms the waters, but that the storm, when we feel that God does not care, and things are out of control, is a time of encounter with Jesus. We need to confront the danger and panic with faith in him. We need to go overboard, let go of the last security of the boat, and walk only by looking steadfastly at Jesus.

It would be easy to moralize. The main value of this miracle for me is the way Matthew presents the close relationship of faith and wonder born of fear.

Glory Revealed

The Transfiguration story presents a different kind of ambiguity in the disciples' sense of wonder, which is characteristic of the experience of holiness in the Old Testament – the tension felt between wonder and fear, the sense of awe as both *tremendum* and *fascinans*, drawing us on as we can be when gripped by something dangerous, and finding ourselves unable to move away.

Matthew 17.1–8

[1]And after six days Jesus took with him Peter and James and John his brother, and led them up a high mountain apart. [2]And he was transfigured before them, and his face shone like the sun, and his garments became white as light. [3]And behold, there appeared to them Moses and Elijah, talking with him. [4]And Peter said to Jesus, 'Lord, it is well that we are here; if you wish, I will make three booths here, one for you and one for Moses and one for Elijah.' [5]He was still speaking, when lo, a bright cloud overshadowed them, and a voice from the cloud said, 'This is my beloved Son, with whom I am well

pleased; listen to him.' ⁶When the disciples heard this, they fell on their faces, and were filled with awe. ⁷But Jesus came and touched them, saying, 'Rise, and have no fear.' ⁸And when they lifted up their eyes, they saw no one but Jesus only.

Peter's comment 'it is well' has also been translated as 'it is wonderful to be here'. But they do not know what to say because they are afraid. Similarly there is a tension between encounter and incomprehension. Again we are invited to consider how much our ability to experience what God is doing is conditioned by our need to understand, and the poverty of our resources for doing so. In Matthew's account (Matthew 17.1–8) Jesus reassures them.

The sequel is no less important. As they come down the mountain, questions are still in their minds; they have missed the point of the miracle, which was to begin teaching the disciples about the mystery of the cross. Only very much later, after the Resurrection had begun to sink in, would they understand.

The Glory of the Resurrection

Mark 16.1–8

¹And when the sabbath was past, Mary Magdalene, and Mary the mother of James, and Salome, bought spices, so that they might go and anoint him. ²And very early on the first day of the week they went to the tomb when the sun had risen. ³And they were saying to one another, 'Who will roll away the stone for us from the door of the tomb?' ⁴And looking up, they saw that the stone was rolled back; – it was very large. ⁵And entering the tomb, they saw a young man sitting on the right side, dressed in a white robe; and they were amazed. ⁶And he said to them, 'Do not be amazed; you seek Jesus of Nazareth, who was crucified. He has risen, he is not here; see the

place where they laid him. [7]But go, tell his disciples and Peter that he is going before you to Galilee; there you will see him, as he told you.' [8]And they went out and fled from the tomb; for trembling and astonishment had come upon them; and they said nothing to any one, for they were afraid.

The story of the Resurrection itself teaches us how wonder is often born of disbelief. In its earliest form, Mark's account of Easter morning probably ended abruptly with the women frightened out of their wits. In Matthew the experience has been reinterpreted as one of awe and great joy. But the Resurrection stories flicker between fear and joy, disbelief and faith, surprise and recognition. The lesson they teach is that in encountering Jesus Christ as God we have to move into a new kind of relationship with him, we have to allow our experience of that to restructure our understanding of life's destiny, even though we have no adequate concepts with which to do so. We are left wondering. This can sometimes be felt as something of a threat, sometimes as too good to be true.

Practical Section

The main part of this chapter has considered how wonder can arise in different kinds of context, indeed how it can emerge from an experience of doubt or fear which initially may not seem a likely context in which to meet God. Wonder too is an ambivalent state: it can be a point, or move us to a point, of discovery of God; but it can be a point at which we turn aside, or refuse to take the step towards discovery. Capacity for wonder is a capacity to be open to God; wonder is a point at which we show ourselves ready either to move towards him in faith and hope, or to close down and turn away.

It is important to try to develop our capacity for wonder, which means being able to let things be, and to admire them for that. People who are good at wondering are likely to be people who can say easily and gladly, 'It takes all sorts', rather than get cross that others are different; or who can laugh at themselves when things do not work out! Wonder means being ready to enjoy something rather than to understand it; we can wonder at a discovery, but it is not our understanding of it that is the reason for our wonder, it is the thing itself. It is a time for thanksgiving and humility, not for self-congratulation. The only way I know how to develop this capacity is to treasure the moments when we find ourselves wondering, and to give them the time and appreciation we have perhaps not given them before. In particular I think it is worth trying to stop panicking when we find ourselves in the dark.

The way to do this is the same as with any kind of panic; we need to be able to relax, to breathe calmly, steadily and deeply, acknowledge the situation and our immediate reaction, but then learn that we can make choices. The choice we need to make is not to run away, or to fight, but to stay calmly in the dark, waiting for the mist to clear, or for our sight to get used to things again, so that we can stay open to what there is to discover.

If we find that we are coming to *lectio* in a difficult patch, it is helpful to take plenty of time, even before starting, just to calm down and tune in to our actual feelings. This is not self-indulgent; it will actually make it easier to listen to the scripture because we will not find the part of us that feels ignored constantly interfering with our *lectio*, claiming attention that it has not yet received. It will also make it possible for us to hear the echoes and resonances we need, perhaps more than ever, to listen to for guidance or reassurance.

Sometimes the moment of wondering can interrupt reading, meditation or prayer. It does not only grow out of the kind of praying talked about earlier. Since *lectio divina* is about allowing a relationship to develop with God, we should not worry about putting the words to one side. But equally we should learn that the scriptures are part of God's way of talking to us, and we should be careful not to neglect the words we have been given. They should help to shape our lives.

A different point is that sometimes we will find that the words of scripture or the meditation we have begun gets in the way of the praying. We need to remember that the four elements of *lectio divina* we have been considering are not discrete steps up a ladder. One leads to another in its own way. Sometimes the movement from reading to wondering can be very quick. We need to learn then that we do not need to do more than use the words to keep ourselves focused on God. The test is whether we can return to reading or meditation without feeling we are turning away from what really matters. It is impossible to meditate when the mind is caught up in something quite different and more important.

In *lectio divina* it is not normally as complicated as that! It is usually just a question of being ready to sit with what we have read, dwelt on and prayed over, just letting the whole thing sink in. To return to the food metaphor introduced for *meditatio*, it is a question of showing respect to our digestion. At the end of a good meal we do not immediately jump up and get on with the next thing. We sit and take time to enjoy the food shared, and especially to enjoy the company in which we have shared the food and drink. It is a time for gratitude, for humour and togetherness.

So it is good not to hurry out of the presence of God we have savoured in our time of prayer. One thing we can do is return to some words to savour them again, but this time less with the thought of what they mean for me, but rather with the thought of who has uttered them, and with what merciful or generous purpose. This is a time just to let God be God, and to let God be God for me. Our own self-offering to God will come naturally out of that.

Chapter Five:
Doing the Word

The movement from *lectio* and prayer to our daily lives was also the subject of reflection in the Middle Ages. The fourfold scheme outlined by the Carthusian monk, Guigo, ended with contemplation. For a monk living in complete solitude within the enclosure of a hermitage that is probably only right; the work of the hermit is completely focused on God. That is not true for very many of us! Like the disciples after the Transfiguration, most of us have to come back down the mountain and resume our normal occupations and responsibilities. But we should not lose heart! The word of God teaches us how close God is to us; in response to him, it is natural for us to bring ourselves to him and to look at our daily lives in relation to him, to pray to him for our needs and be thankful for the life we draw from him. In particular we can begin to find the Holy Spirit, or rather signs of the Spirit's presence, in our life, as well as to recognize the pull of other influences and 'spirits' which draw us away from following the Lord with our whole hearts and see them for what they are. In this way the word of God can become a principle of discernment as to how God is moving in our lives, sharing with us his gifts, inviting, suggesting, even directing us in our lives of faith.

It is not much use trying to think of prayer and contemplation as getting out of ourselves, or rising above the changes and chances of this world of ours. There is no escape; and this is where God saves us. Perhaps we have rather to learn to get back into ourselves, and this would be a more truthful way to pray. *Lectio divina* ought to be able to help us here. It helps us discover the true ground of our life as ground God has given us and on which he meets us; *lectio divina* helps us learn how good it is for us to be here. The demands facing us are probably very ordinary too, but no less challenging for that. Perhaps all we need is to begin to see that what we do in the most ordinary sort of way in looking after our families and in our job of work has its precious part to play in the life of the Gospel. Perhaps our job is simply, but no less like the disciples after the Resurrection, to be bearers of good tidings to the people we know only too well, to encourage, console, forgive and make peace.

A traditional way in which the practical consequences of *lectio divina* were thought through had three stages, tracing an outward movement from *lectio divina* back to our daily life. It started with a process of discernment of the Spirit in regard to the practical needs and demands of my life (*discretio*); this led to a moment of decision, a choice of God's will for me as it seems to my conscience to be (*deliberatio*); this naturally embodied itself in faithful action (*actio*). We can consider this process a bit more closely.

Discernment helps us appreciate the presence of the Spirit in our own lives. This invites us to reflect on the idea of the Gifts of the Spirit. The traditional list is based on Isaiah 11.2. There the Spirit of the Lord is spoken of as a spirit of wisdom and understanding, of counsel and might, a spirit of knowledge and the fear of the Lord. These gifts have a lot to do with our 'heads' – wisdom, understanding and so on – but also to do with our wills – might or courage – and our hearts – a sense of reverence and the fear of the Lord. These gifts engage with the way we look at things, with the way we make decisions and the way we live them out.

The Spirit helps us to understand things truly, by helping us to see them as God sees them. It helps us to be more keenly aware of good and bad, of right and wrong, and so to be more in tune with the will of God. In helping us to understand this and to make decisions accordingly, the Spirit helps us follow the path of discipleship courageously, and to be sensitive to the presence of God in the world, in other people and in our own hearts. Gifts need to be unwrapped and used. These are gifts we should use in the service of God. When we make use of them, they are transformational: the Spirit that makes all things new raises our minds and hearts; he redirects our lives to live towards God and towards others. It is something of which *lectio divina* can make us more aware, because it gives us the time consciously to engage with the Holy Spirit and to pray how to respond to him.

But this involves a moment of choice, decisions based on our understanding of God's will. In this connection we can reflect on the passages where Jesus talks of the need to discern the signs of his Kingdom, to consider what the Spirit is doing around us. Some of our reflection on scripture in *meditatio* ought to allow room for that, and that will lead in turn to prayer, especially the prayer of intercession. This is a precious ministry of prayer, of which the Old and New Testaments give many examples. It may find us wrestling with God, like Jacob, or pleading with him, like Moses, as well as humbly bowing ourselves down before God as Job did after his indignant protest at undeserved suffering. But always such prayer should be accompanied by the offering of ourselves to God's service, so that his will be done in us and that we may do his will. Intercession includes a call to discipleship.

Certainly such prayer will help us understand how God is addressing us in our lives. It will help us face up to the way he is calling us to serve him; it will help us derive confidence and hope. For me this is the meaning of *deliberatio*. We must remember that this kind of thinking about our lives should still be understood as a movement of prayer; it is not simply a reflection at a practical level about Christian life. But this kind of prayer takes us beyond our reading, and the immediate contact with God it has revealed, into action. It helps us live our lives prayerfully.

However it may be, Christians need to consider how the conduct of their lives is being formed by the word of God. How do I, in actual fact, reflect the image of God that I see in Jesus Christ? *Lectio* is an attempt to root our faith, hope and love of God not only in our attention to his word and in our desire for him, but also in our seeking to do his will.

Contemplation on the word of God has both an inward and an outward movement. The Spirit leads us inwards to the word of God, to prayer and communion with Christ and adoration of the Father; but he also draws us back to ourselves and to our fellow human beings. It is not enough to contemplate; we should share the fruits of our contemplation with others.

The rest of this chapter is about being practical, so there is no practical section to end it. The passages for reflection begin with the insistence in the scriptures on putting the word of God into practice, and the dangers of not doing so. They talk about the spiritual wisdom that really enables us to live out the word of God, and which means learning to have the mind of Christ. The mind of Christ is one that is animated by the Spirit, and it is in this context that we can best think about *discretio* and *deliberatio*. These will be discussed as separate sections in what follows.

Be Doers of the Word

The following passage of the Letter of James puts things as directly as possible. A living faith means acting on the word we receive. Not to do so is self-deception.

James 1.19–25

[19]Know this, my beloved brothers and sisters. Let everyone be quick to hear, slow to speak, slow to anger, [20]for the anger of a human being does not work the righteousness of God. [21]Therefore put away all filthiness and rank growth of wickedness and receive with meekness the implanted word, which is able to save your souls. [22]But be doers of the word, and not hearers only, deceiving yourselves. [23]For everyone that is a hearer of the word and not a doer, they are like people who observe their natural face in a mirror; [24]they observe themselves and go away and at once forget what they were like. [25]But everyone who looks into the perfect law, the law of liberty, and

perseveres, being no hearer that forgets but a doer that acts, shall be blessed in their doing.

How quickly do we listen? That is to say, how readily do we put aside our own conversations and preoccupations to let someone else have their say? Does God get any better reception? James sees a close link between talking, anger and violence. Certainly when we are angry it is particularly hard to stop and listen. And yet if we did, perhaps we would be able to see a bigger picture than ourselves, and that would be a first step to the understanding that lets peace grow.

There are times, to be sure, when it is right to be angry, and James is perhaps alert to this when he says we should be *slow* about it. It is too easy to be angry unjustly or to misdirect our anger: to make just judgements we need to be quick to listen to God's word, and ready to let it shape our feelings.

It may be that we need to allow *lectio divina* to help us listen to our suppressed anger (often expressed in sadness); in order for the word to reach us properly we need to be honest. The word of God can give that courage and self-knowledge, just as it can guide our response to it. James also sees that self-assertiveness needs to be put aside so that we may be meek enough to listen to God who is never self-assertive when he addresses us. But meekness does not mean inertia: the word of God can bring us to ourselves *so that* we do what is right and just.

The word is planted in us. The image reminds us of the parable of the Sower. We have to clear the soil of the rank growth of wickedness; we have to receive the seed of the word. But God is the one who plants, who cultivates. The word bears fruit in our lives.

The image of the person looking at himself in the mirror is a telling one. Mirrors are not there to be looked at themselves, but to reflect an image of the person looking. The scriptures do reveal us to ourselves. They enable us to grow in self-knowledge. But they also reveal what we could look like. In Jesus they show us how God lives human life; the rest of the scriptures explore the possibilities of human life in its glory and in its disgrace. Finding ourselves in the picture helps us make choices about what kind of person we are trying to be. We may not like what we see, we may quail at the challenge. But the word is also a spirit-filled word of power that helps us grow in God's grace, and live according to his will.

In contrast to a living faith showing itself in action, Jesus talks about those who do not live according to the word they have received. These are the 'hypocrites'. The Greek word means actor; hypocrites are just going through the motions, pretending to be what they are not, essentially empty masks. They are very judgemental – in psychological terms, full of projection: they criticize as failure in others what they are themselves failing to be. *Lectio divina* is a gentle way of looking at ourselves honestly, because the one who shows us who we are is the Father who loves us.

Matthew 7.1–5, 16–21, 24–27

[1]'Judge not, that you be not judged. [2]For with the judgment you pronounce you will be judged, and the measure you give will be the measure you get. [3]Why do you see the speck that is in your fellow human being's eye, but do not notice the log that is in your own eye? [4]Or how can you say to your fellow human being, "Let me take the speck out of your eye," when there is the log in your own eye? [5]You hypocrite, first take the log out of your own eye, and then you will see clearly to take the speck out of theirs. . . .

[16]'You will know them by their fruits. Are grapes gathered from thorns, or figs from thistles? [17]So, every sound tree bears good fruit, but the bad tree bears evil fruit. [18]A sound tree cannot bear evil

fruit, nor can a bad tree bear good fruit. [19]Every tree that does not bear good fruit is cut down and thrown into the fire. [20]Thus you will know them by their fruits.

[21]'Not every one who says to me, "Lord, Lord," shall enter the kingdom of heaven, but he who does the will of my Father who is in heaven. . . .

[24]'Every one then who hears these words of mine and does them will be like a wise man who built his house upon the rock; [25]and the rain fell, and the floods came, and the winds blew and beat upon that house, but it did not fall, because it had been founded on the rock. [26]And every one who hears these words of mine and does not do them will be like a foolish man who built his house upon the sand; [27]and the rain fell, and the floods came, and the winds blew and beat against that house, and it fell; and great was the fall of it.'

This long section from the Sermon on the Mount – and there are others – always makes sobering reading. As rational creatures we have to make judgements, of course. The problem is how do we judge, positively or negatively? Do we judge as God judges, mercifully eager to justify and to support? Or do we just find fault, disparage, put down – and all that? Do we put ourselves above others or alongside them, let alone at their service?

In this passage hypocrites are people who think they can begin the work of judgement anywhere else than with themselves. They do not look at themselves in the mirror in order to take the log out of their eye! Some radical changes of outlook are required of us here. To make them is to grow in the wisdom that comes down from above. Living by the word probably means beginning to change oneself, before starting to worry too much about others.

Always the test of what is going on is our love, the kind of fruit we are bearing in our lives. As Jesus says elsewhere, it is a matter of deeds rather than words. We cannot ever be sure whether we are doing God's will or really just glorifying our own, except by the test of what kind of fruit our lives are bearing. Does it come from above or below?

Taking the word of God to heart, building our lives according to what we learn from him, is to give our lives a sure foundation. The word becomes a source of wisdom. We are able to build our house on the rock – the rock, as St Paul understood it, that is Christ (1 Corinthians 10.5).

Wisdom from Above

James speaks of a wisdom from above, a wisdom that helps us see things as God sees them, and to want the things God wants.

James 3.13–18

[13]Who is wise and understanding among you? By their good lives let them show their works in the meekness of wisdom. [14]But if you have bitter jealousy and selfish ambition in your hearts, do not boast and be false to the truth. [15]This wisdom is not such as comes down from above, but is earthly, unspiritual, devilish. [16]For where jealousy and selfish ambition exist, there will be disorder and every vile practice. [17]But the wisdom from above is first pure, then peaceable, gentle, open to reason, full of mercy and good fruits, without uncertainty or insincerity. [18]And the harvest of righteousness is sown in peace by those who make peace.

James contrasts two kinds of wisdom, an earthly 'wisdom' or know-how governed by the spirit of getting on in the world regardless, and the wisdom from above, which is shown by its fruits.

The Mind of Christ

There are other passages in the New Testament that introduce the two contrasting sets of values. In 1 Corinthians, for instance, Paul contrasts the true wisdom of the cross with the wisdom of this age; and in the same passage, he talks of the Holy Spirit as that which reaches to the very heart of God and reveals God's meaning to us. It endows us with the mind of Christ. This is a wisdom that expresses itself in sacrificial living, where we embrace the mystery of the cross in our own lives.

1 Corinthians 2.9–16

[9]But, as it is written, 'What no eye has seen, nor ear heard, nor the heart of man conceived, what God has prepared for those who love him,' [10]God has revealed to us through the Spirit. For the Spirit searches everything, even the depths of God. [11]For what person knows a person's thoughts except the spirit of the person in them? So also no one comprehends the thoughts of God except the Spirit of God. [12]Now we have received not the spirit of the world, but the Spirit which is from God, that we might understand the gifts bestowed on us by God. [13]And we impart this in words not taught by human wisdom but taught by the Spirit, interpreting spiritual truths to those who possess the Spirit. [14]Unspiritual people do not receive the gifts of the Spirit of God, for they are folly to them, and they are not able to understand them because they are spiritually discerned. [15]Spiritual people judge all things, but are themselves to be judged by no one. [16]'For who has known the mind of the Lord so as to instruct him?' But we have the mind of Christ.

Paul's line of thought here appeals to a kind of correspondence between God's Spirit and our spirit: our spirit is made to communicate with God's Spirit. The spirit is what gives life to our hearts, deeper than our emotional life. The idea of spirit here is a kind of self-understanding; it knows our own thoughts, but it is something deeper than our minds, even at their most intuitive level of activity. It is the principle of our life; in the Christian way of looking at human life, our life is not fundamentally a biological reality, and the spirit is not just a biological power.

Fundamentally we are spiritual creatures, created by God for communion with him. Our spirit, then, is the level of our personal life that looks towards God who is spirit. At the level of the spirit we are in communication with ourselves and with God – at least potentially: for we only know God in so far as he makes himself known, again at the level of the spirit, through the Holy Spirit. *Lectio divina* helps us find ourselves at home at this level of awareness: for it is in our response to the word of God that the Holy Spirit, at work in our hearts as we listen as well as in the inspired words we listen to, makes himself known.

For Paul, the critical question is what we are tuned into at the level of the spirit. Do we listen to the spirit of this world, or to God who has made us for himself? The world's vanity and pride hangs around like an unpleasant smell hanging in the fresh air. We sense it as a distraction, a tension, if not a conflict, in our spirit between the attraction of a fallen world and God. The latter is a source of true wisdom, the former ultimately fraudulent, leaving us unspiritual people, our minds dominated by the world-minus-God, what Paul calls the 'flesh'.

But when we open our minds and hearts to God, our spirit can share in the wisdom of the Holy Spirit. For God's Spirit, who animates the whole of creation, goes to the depths of our hearts too. He gifts our natural life with new, godly life. These are the Gifts of the Spirit that were mentioned in the introduction to this chapter. By these gifts our minds are renewed; we learn to think the way God thinks, and love what he loves. We learn to have the mind of Christ.

Romans 12.1–2

[1]I appeal to you therefore, brothers and sisters, by the mercies of God, to present your bodies as a living sacrifice, holy and acceptable to God, which is your spiritual worship. [2]Do not be conformed to

this world but be transformed by the renewal of your mind, that you may prove what is the will of God, what is good and acceptable and perfect.

Lectio divina should indeed give us a sense of the mercies of God, so that we begin to see our lives as part of the mystery of redemption that culminated in Christ's sacrifice of himself on the cross. The gift of our own lives is thus only a measure of our gratitude, an appreciation of all that God has given us. It is our only fitting worship. But in offering such a gift, we are changed and able to become agents of change, and share with Christ in the renewal of all things.

Discretio

God's Spirit enables us to distinguish between the 'smell' of the world and the smell of God's fresh air. He helps us understand how God is at work in our lives, and how, in the midst of conflicting pressures and impulses, we can try to respond to the God-given possibility of growth. This process is what, from the very beginning, the monks called the discernment of spirits. Discernment (from the Latin verb *discernere*) means the ability to tell the difference between good and evil, two forces of attraction at work that are often hard to detect. But an awareness of God's presence in our hearts helps show things up as they really are. This is another way of thinking about what it is to have the 'mind of Christ'. The light of Christ's word shines in the darkness (John 1.4–5), and the darkness can never quench it! We can compare the words of Jesus, that his disciples need to be lights that can shine so that people can see, and no longer need to walk in darkness (Matthew 5.14–16). As we learn to make the Spirit the principle of our lives, thought and action, we will begin to radiate light for others and find ourselves entering into the dynamic of growth that makes us fully human, like Christ, begotten by God for new and eternal life.

Test the spirits

1 John 4.1–3a

[1]Beloved, do not believe every spirit, but test the spirits to see whether they are of God ... [2]By this you know the Spirit of God: every spirit that confesses Jesus Christ has come in the flesh is of God, [3]and every spirit that does not confess Jesus is not of God.

St Benedict in his Rule used this short passage to preface his discussion of recruitment and formation in the monastic life. Its simple and fundamental message is that Jesus, and our faith in his divine authority and incarnation, is central to our knowing God's will. Whatever is on our mind, we need to set it against the standard of Christ. In the old days the question was 'what would Jesus have done?', or 'what would he do?' This is not necessarily the best question to ask, but we can certainly consider how well a course of action, a project or a concern fits in with our knowledge of Christ. More is often needed than just a literal doing what the Bible says, and *lectio divina* is a good way to develop the kind of familiarity with Jesus we need to 'fit' the words of the Bible to the particular circumstances of our lives. We need wisdom, not literal-mindedness.

Set your minds on the Spirit

Romans 8 is the great chapter on the Holy Spirit. This is not the place to explain where this chapter fits in the overall argument of this most theologically dense of Paul's writings. All that need be said is that here we see Paul presenting the Holy Spirit as the great moving force in the new creation by which we become children of God, sharing the life of his own Son, and able to call God 'Abba', Father. Because we have been brought to new life in Christ, Paul argues we should learn a new way of thinking, setting our minds on the things of the Spirit. He is well aware of the inner struggle this involves, but he also knows that the Spirit comes to the help of our weakness, and helps us re-centre our lives on God and not on ourselves.

Romans 8.5–6

[5]For those who live according to the flesh set their minds on the things of the flesh, but those who live according to the Spirit set their minds on the things of the Spirit. [6]To set the mind on the flesh is death, but to set the mind on the Spirit is life and peace.

Paul adds here to the line of thought introduced in 1 Corinthians 2.9–16 (see above) the blunt contrast between the flesh and spirit in terms of death and life. The two ways of thinking are death-bound or orientated towards life. But this is also a diagnostic tool. We can discern the spirits in so far as they are looking in one direction or the other. Of course we can deceive ourselves but, if we are truly seeking the wisdom that comes from above, our *lectio divina* can help us reach good conclusions about this. No judgement at this level is infallible, of course, but with continued listening and prayer we can make conscientious, if provisional, decisions.

Certainly the mark of the Spirit is peace. Not that peace is always won without a struggle, for Jesus made peace by shedding his blood on the cross (Colossians 1.20). So it is not a question of the right thing being the one that makes us feel most comfortable. But if in our *lectio divina* we find ourselves increasingly conscious of a sense of dis-ease, I think we can suspect that this does not lie in the path that leads to peace, and have good reason to be cautious.

A spirit of Sonship

St Paul's expression in Romans 8.15 refers to our having the status of sons. Inclusive versions render this as 'adoption'. I feel that something important is lost in dropping the reference to sonship. For Paul, we are God's children because we are reborn and adopted *in Jesus*, God's only Son: by grace, we share his own specific relation to his Father as the only-begotten Son, the Beloved, and raised to life in him. There is only one who is begotten from the Father. Because we are members of his Body, we share in his Spirit.

Romans 8.14–17

[14]For all who are led by the Spirit of God are children of God. [15]For you did not receive the spirit of slavery to fall back into fear, but you have received the spirit of Sonship. When we cry, 'Abba! Father!' [16]it is the Spirit himself bearing witness with our spirit that we are children of God, [17]and if children, then heirs, heirs of God and fellow heirs with Christ, provided we suffer with him in order that we may also be glorified with him.

Certainly we have to review our lives within the dynamic of Trinitarian life, which we enter by grace and by the power of the Spirit in our lives. The Spirit will surely be moving us in such a way that we can become more fully integrated into the movement of love that unites Father, Son and Spirit. So here Paul develops the thought about freedom we were considering before: a sign of spiritual discernment will be the sense of fear or of adoption, of enslavement (in whatever sense) or of freedom. Not that that will be an easy option either. Part of the dynamic of Trinitarian life in this world is the drama of the cross. Perhaps we do not look for the sign of the cross enough.

The Spirit helps us in our weakness

Romans 7.14–25

[14]We know that the law is spiritual; but I am carnal, sold under sin. [15]I do not understand my own actions. For I do not do what I

want, but I do the very thing I hate. [16]Now if I do what I do not want, I agree that the law is good. [17]So then it is no longer I that do it, but sin which dwells within me. [18]For I know that nothing good dwells within me, that is, in my flesh. I can will what is right, but I cannot do it. [19]For I do not do the good I want, but the evil I do not want is what I do. [20]Now if I do what I do not want, it is no longer I that do it, but sin which dwells within me. [21]So I find it to be a law that when I want to do right, evil lies close at hand. [22]For I delight in the law of God, in my inmost self, [23]but I see in my members another law at war with the law of my mind and making me captive to the law of sin which dwells in my members. [24]Wretched human being that I am! Who will deliver me from this body of death? [25]Thanks be to God through Jesus Christ our Lord! So then, I of myself serve the law of God with my mind, but with my flesh I serve the law of sin.

We should not be surprised at the continued effort we find we have to make to follow God's will. The drama of our redemption is never completed in this life: but the Spirit and the flesh continue to pull in their different directions, and the tension runs right through the core of our being. The remarkable thing is that this is good for us as it strengthens our dependence on God's work in our hearts. We must constantly return to the inner delight we find in God's word. This is a testimony to the power of the Spirit in our inmost being. Paul notes that God works not only through Jesus Christ who redeems us, but also, at the start of chapter 8, he introduces the Holy Spirit, the 'Spirit of life in Christ Jesus' who continually prays in us and for us (Romans 8.26–30). For everything works together for good for those who love God.

So there should be a growth in humility and a readiness to turn thankfully to God through Jesus Christ rather than a sense of self-disgust or hatred. The test as to which is the ruling power

in our life, the Spirit or sin, is simply whether or not we delight in the law of God.

Be led by the Spirit and discern its fruits

The previous passages have given a sense of the big picture, the dynamic of life in Christ as the context within which we have to test the spirits and discern the will of God. This final passage, from Galatians, gives specific criteria by which we can discern the will of God.

Galatians 5.16–26

[16]But I say, walk by the Spirit, and do not gratify the desires of the flesh. [17]For the desires of the flesh are against the Spirit, and the desires of the Spirit are against the flesh; for these are opposed to each other, to prevent you from doing what you would. [18]But if you are led by the Spirit you are not under the law. [19]Now the works of the flesh are plain: fornication, impurity, licentiousness, [20]idolatry, sorcery, enmity, strife, jealousy, anger, selfishness, dissension, party spirit, [21]envy, drunkenness, carousing, and the like. I warn you, as I warned you before, that those who do such things shall not inherit the kingdom of God. [22]But the fruit of the Spirit is love, joy, peace, patience, kindness, goodness, faithfulness, [23]gentleness, self-control; against such there is no law. [24]And those who belong to Christ Jesus have crucified the flesh with its passions and desires. [25]If we live by the Spirit, let us also walk by the Spirit. [26]Let us have no self-conceit, no provoking of one another, no envy of one another.

There are many points for reflection here. Paul begins by contrasting the Spirit as something by which we walk; the desires of the flesh are a distraction, but the implication here is that they do not lead anywhere! They are just self-gratification. The second point is that, consistent with what we have already seen, following the path of the Spirit, or fulfilling his desires,

is ultimately doing what we really want to do – a hazardous criterion in itself, but an instructive observation: what do we really want?

It is often a revealing exercise in praying about something to begin by wanting God, and getting ourselves as aware as we can be how wanting God can be a hunger of our whole being. Then see what happens to all the other wants we may have. It is a very healthy exercise in getting things in perspective and proportion. The fact that we are doing this as part of a faithful practice of *lectio divina* is an important corrective against self-deception, but also an encouragement that the Spirit will guide us to know the truth.

The list of the fruits of the Spirit is preceded by a more frightening list of works of the flesh. We need to remember that by the flesh, Paul means a human nature that is not animated by the Holy Spirit, human life unredeemed by Christ. The list describes rather deep-rooted problems that prevent our being completely open to the Spirit. At their most deeply ingrained, I am afraid they tend to kill the life of the Spirit, and close our hearts to God.

These problems are not exact opposites of the list of fruits. But if we were to think through a list of opposites to the fruits of the Spirit, we would have a list that describes a distressingly familiar world: hatred, despair, violence, impatience, unkindness, mean-heartedness, unfaithfulness, hardness, lack of self-control! This is the way our spiritual environment is being polluted. We ought to ask what the sources of the pollution are. What is the extent of our own responsibility?

Conversely the list of fruits of the Spirit gives a positive diagnostic. We should rejoice at them, and see how evil can be overcome with good. Any course of action that promises to enable these qualities of life to flourish is highly likely to be one in which the Spirit is able to flourish.

Deliberatio

Perhaps we can distinguish *discretio* from *deliberatio* to some extent like this: *discretio* is a consideration of the movement of the spirit in my life, the tension between the pull of God's Spirit and my attraction or attachment to other sources of motivation; *deliberatio*, on the other hand, is a wider consideration of what God is doing in the broader circumstances of my life and the world around me. *Discretio* helps me tune in to God's call: *deliberatio* helps me make a choice for God more faithfully.

Reading the signs of the times

Jesus talks about the signs of the times. He is replying to the Jews who were asking him to prove his claims by some sign. He protests that the problem is that they cannot read the signs that are already evident if they knew how to look.

Matthew 16.1–3

[1]And the Pharisees and Sadducees came, and to test him they asked him to show them a sign from heaven. [2]He answered them, 'When it is evening, you say, "It will be fair weather, for the sky is red." [3]And in the morning, "It will be stormy today, for the sky is red and threatening." You know how to interpret the appearance of the sky, but you cannot interpret the signs of the times.'

The Pharisees and Sadducees can read one kind of sign, but not another; they can see the physical meaning of things, but not the spiritual meaning. This is what we try to learn by *lectio divina*. The word Jesus uses for 'times' is *kairoi*, with its meaning of a critical moment, a time of decision; in the New Testament it has the sense of time according to God's rhythm and pace of doing things, rather than against the clock. In his parallel version, Luke (12.54–56) puts it a little differently when Jesus says we cannot interpret the present time. We need to be able to read the

present time as part of God's time, and not just look for significant elements of the present situation as indicators of God's purposes. To be able to interpret that means being able to understand God's purpose, his sense of timing; it demands faith, and a sense of God's perspective.

In fact, in Matthew's Gospel, Jesus says we have been given a sign, but have overlooked it. He talks of the 'sign of Jonah' (16.4). This cryptic comment can be read in two ways. It can be seen as a prophecy of the passion of Jesus, like Jonah, who stayed in the belly of the whale for three days and nights. This is the sense given at Matthew 12.39. But it can also refer to Jesus' ministry of preaching. Jonah preached God's judgement on Nineveh and the people repented, and were forgiven. This is the sense intended at Matthew 12.38–42 and Luke 11.29–32. Both meanings are relevant to *deliberatio* about our own times. For we need to recognize God's judgement on our society and be prepared to call for justice, as well as witness to divine compassion and his readiness to forgive. We also have to be ready to find hope in the Paschal shape of so much suffering in our world, and try to ensure that it is not fruitless, but that it can be a path to resurrection and new life.

In many places in the New Testament the word *kairos* is used to refer to the fullness of time, the time of redemption (Mark 1.15). For example, Jesus is reproached by the devils he casts out as coming before the time (Matthew 8.29). The question we have to ask and pray about is how are we called to make Jesus present, and be sources of redemption today. That would be our response to the sign of Jonah.

Make the most of the time

Discernment of the time, or of the Spirit, should naturally express itself in decision. Jesus can be quite categorical about the choices we need to make. He turns no one away, but he challenges everyone. The same Jesus who says his yoke is easy and his burden light (Matthew 11.28–30) also says that it is a narrow path that leads to life and few there are who find it (Matthew 7.13–14).

Ephesians 5.8–11, 15–17

[8]Once you were darkness, but now you are light in the Lord; walk as children of the light [9](for the fruit of the light is found in all that is good and right and true), [10]and try to learn what is pleasing to the Lord. [11]Take no part in the unfruitful works of darkness, but instead expose them. . . .

[15]Look carefully then how you walk, not as unwise but as wise, [16]making the most of the time, because the days are evil. [17]Therefore do not be foolish but understand what the will of the Lord is.

Lectio divina is our way of finding the light shed by God's word (Psalm 119.105). In *deliberatio* we bring our lives into the light of that word. Prayer helps us discover what is pleasing to the Lord. Here Paul suggests three fundamental criteria of that: what is good, right and true.

Truth is a big idea in the Bible – but we can at least begin with honesty, particularly in the more profound sense of personal integrity. We lead such fragmented lives, and so many impulses of modern culture encourage the idea of fragmentation. Prayer is sometimes the only place we have to bring ourselves back together, sometimes a slow and painful process. It teaches us, perhaps as well as anything, that truth is a quality of life we discover face to face with God, the source and sustainer of our lives, in whom we live and move and have our being (Acts 17.28). For the Bible teaches us that truth is a fundamental characteristic of God; it expresses his faithfulness and commitment to creation; it is generally linked to the Hebrew word for his merciful loving-kindness. So truth, as something we are confronted with in our meditation on the word of God, encompasses the integrity of our relationships with God and with the whole of creation. It should invite some searching questions on our part!

In the New Testament, especially in the Gospel of John, truth takes on a personal character: Jesus is the way, the truth, and the life (John 14.6). The Holy Spirit leads us into all truth (John 16.13). Truth, in this richest sense, is something we know because we have let Jesus' word make us part of the truthfulness of God. It engages us with God's own compassion and faithfulness with mankind.

Come, follow me

Perhaps the most important dimension of the choices we have to make is the vocational dimension, learning to discern the Spirit as hearing Jesus' call to follow him.

Mark 10.17–22

[17]And as he was setting out on his journey, a man ran up and knelt before him, and asked him, 'Good Teacher, what must I do to inherit eternal life?' [18]and Jesus said to him, 'Why do you call me good? No one is good but God alone. [19]You know the commandments: "Do not kill, Do not commit adultery, Do not steal, Do not bear false witness, Do not defraud, Honour your father and mother".' [20]And he said to him, 'Teacher, all these I have observed from my youth.' [21]And Jesus looking upon him loved him, and said to him, 'You lack one thing; go, sell what you have, and give to the poor, and you will have treasure in heaven; and come, follow me.' [22]At that saying his countenance fell, and he went away sorrowful; for he had great possessions.

The story is told in all the Synoptic Gospels; Mark adds the detail of Jesus looking at the young man and loving him. He can see the man's good will. His problem is not that he has done

133

anything wrong, nor that he is falling short in any straightforward way. What he lacks is perhaps something of the spontaneity of the Lord's love, its generosity, a readiness to think not in terms of this world, but in terms of treasure in heaven.

It is a challenge for all of us. Thinking about what we ought to do, about what is right and good, needs to take us beyond moral rules in the ordinary sense. This leaves us a fair space to do what we like within what is permissible. Jesus invites us to shape our lives in terms of our commitments to other people, and above all to him. Love knows no bounds (cf. 1 Corinthians 13.8): the beauty of that whole passage at once encourages us, but it must also challenge us.

The story ends with Jesus' invitation to discipleship, and the stark lesson that material things can be an obstacle to our following Jesus; so much so that even the disciples who have left everything to follow Jesus despair of anyone being saved. To this, Jesus' reply that we have to depend utterly on God's grace (Mark 10.27) teaches us that the real difficulty is our ingrained need for security, for autonomy, for self-justification. These are things over which we need to reflect prayerfully as we consider how Jesus is calling us to follow him.

The power of service

The disciples clearly did not get the message. At once, as Jesus tells them of his imminent passion and death, they are arguing about status and rewards. The irony is that their slowness can be an encouragement to us: it takes a long time to understand how central the cross is to our Lord's life, let alone to ours. Instructive is our Lord's response:

Mark 10.41–45

[41]And when the ten heard it, they began to be indignant at James and John. [42]And Jesus called them to him and said to them, 'You know

that those who are supposed to rule over the Gentiles lord it over them, and their great men exercise authority over them. [43]But it shall not be so among you; but whoever would be great among you must be your servant, [44]and whoever would be first among you must be slave of all. [45]For the Son of Man did not come to be served but to serve, and to give his life as a ransom for many.'

We must let Jesus teach us a completely new approach to power, the power of love, rather than the power of strength; the power that comes from letting God work through us, rather than thinking we can do it on our own resources. We perhaps also need to drop any romantic ideas about the meaning of love in this context; it means giving way before another, putting ourselves out for them, serving them.

Luke gives this saying of Jesus in the context of the Last Supper (Luke 22.24–27), when he stripped himself of his garments and took on the role of a slave, washing the feet of his disciples. The poignancy of that setting reminds us that we follow Jesus not by imitating the big drama of the cross and Resurrection, but by putting ourselves at the feet of others in need.

Trust in me

Perhaps at a more basic level still we need to learn to trust in God. Time and time again in St John's Gospel Jesus asks us to trust in him (for example, John 14.1); it is the absolute basis of discipleship. The following passage from Matthew's Gospel helps explore the problem:

Matthew 6.25–34

[25]'Therefore I tell you, do not be anxious about your life, what you shall eat or what you shall drink, nor about your body, what you shall put on. Is not life more than food, and the body more than clothing? [26]Look at the birds of the air: they neither sow nor reap nor gather

into barns, and yet your heavenly Father feeds them. Are you not of more value than they? [27]And which of you by being anxious can add one cubit to his span of life? [28]And why are you anxious about clothing? Consider the lilies of the field, how they grow; they neither toil nor spin; [29]yet I tell you, even Solomon in all his glory was not arrayed like one of these. [30]But if God so clothes the grass of the field, which today is alive and tomorrow is thrown into the oven, will he not much more clothe you, O you of little faith? [31]Therefore do not be anxious, saying, 'What shall we eat?' or 'What shall we drink?' or 'What shall we wear?' [32]For the Gentiles seek all these things; and your heavenly Father knows that you need them all. [33]But seek first his kingdom and his righteousness, and all these things shall be yours as well. [34]Therefore do not be anxious about tomorrow, for tomorrow will be anxious for itself. Let the day's own trouble be sufficient for the day.'

Here Jesus contrasts our material anxieties with what is really and lastingly important, the Kingdom of God and his right-eousness. But more than remind us of the true priorities of our lives, Jesus invites us to see how our loss of perspective springs from anxiety; worry makes us unable to see the truth. I often find *lectio divina* lets me realize how anxious I am about so many things, when only one thing is important (Luke 10.42). And Jesus goes one better, and tries to show us that we simply do not need to worry, because God cares. My anxiety is the obverse of my lack of trust; a lack of hope leaves me without courage, unable to let the Holy Spirit take my fear away and replace it with God's love. *Lectio divina* can help here, not because of what I have read or meditated on, but because it has given me the chance to return to the place where I can hear Jesus reassuring me and sharing his Spirit with me just for friendship's sake.

To encourage us, Jesus invites us to look. What could be simpler? But how hard it is just to look at things as they are rather than to see what we expect or fear! What assumptions do we make about things? How ready are we to learn from the way things are? We shape our sense of reality after our own image, rather than let it teach us how things are, including ourselves; how we are always in God's hands. We can know everything there is to know about lilies and the birds of the air, and yet fail to see them, and fail to have discovered our communion with them, and God's creativity that enables them to be, and us to see. Perhaps this is a conversion of consciousness we need if we are to read the signs of God's time and to be for others as he is for us.

A large part of that conversion of consciousness is to learn to live in the present, rather than let our minds be haunted by the unreality of memories of the past, and fantasies about the future. Now is where we are, and where God is. It is the only place where we will discover the richness of communion with him and the joy of living for him.

The perennial beauty of this passage, I think, is the way it relaxes us into choosing God. If only it were always easy just to let go!

Pressing on to the goal

Philippians 3.8–15

[8]Indeed I count everything as loss because of the surpassing worth of knowing Christ Jesus my Lord. For his sake I have suffered the loss of all things, and count them as refuse, in order that I may gain Christ and [9]be found in him, not having a righteousness of my own, based on law, but that which is through faith in Christ, the righteousness from God that depends on faith; [10]that I may know him and the power of his resurrection, and may share his sufferings, becoming like him in his death, [11]that if possible I may attain the resurrection from the dead.

¹²Not that I have already obtained this or am already perfect; but I press on to make it my own, because Christ has made me his own. ¹³ Brethren, I do not consider that I have made it my own; but one thing I do, forgetting what lies behind and straining forward to what lies ahead, ¹⁴ I press on toward the goal for the prize of the upward call of God in Christ Jesus. ¹⁵ Let those who are mature be thus minded.

The call is 'upwards': not just to follow Jesus on earth, but also to be united with him in heaven. It means being ready to let everything go for the sake of what is really important, the 'prize' of 'gaining Christ'.

As so often in Christian life there is a tension between 'now' and 'not yet', between our salvation assured by our faith, and the need to put that faith into practice, the final assurance of being with Christ for ever. We belong to Christ, but we are not yet fully his; we are not yet 'found in him', as if people who were looking for us actually found Jesus! We are not yet living his life to the full, although Paul warns us that this means sharing his passion as part of what it means to share his resurrection.

This is the goal of Christian life, Christian life lived to the full, faith completely realized in action. This is the subject for our last chapter.

Chapter Six:
Living by the Word

St Benedict opens his Rule for monks with the instruction: 'Listen, my son, to the words of the master and incline the ear of your heart; gladly receive the advice of a loving father and faithfully fulfil it, so that by the labour of obedience you may return to him from whom you have strayed by the sloth of disobedience.' The Prologue continues to present the life of a monk as a continual response to the scriptures (Prologue 8–10): 'Let us get up then at last, as the scriptures are waking us with the words "it is high time now for us to get up from our sleep", and with our eyes opened to the divine light let us listen with astonished ears to the instructions that the divine voice calls out to us every day, "Today if you hear his voice, harden not your hearts." ' In the Foreword, this book began by reflecting on the way the Rule understands the divine voice as an invitation to discover true life, offered to everyone who cares to hear. To accept the invitation is to undertake a radical change of direction in our lives, and a new way of living them. The monk is following our Lord who leads us by means of the Gospel (Prologue 21): 'So let us gird up our loins with faith and the observance of good deeds, and let us proceed along his path under the leadership of the Gospel, so that we may deserve to see him who has called us into his kingdom.' St Benedict completes his Prologue by introducing the idea of the monastery as a school where people may learn to do this, a place where the word of God may be put into practice. But the way of life he envisages, although it may include some strictness, is primarily one of personal growth and happiness, holding out to those who start out on the path the ultimate hope of glory: 'By growth in our way of life and in faith, and with our hearts enlarged, we may run in the indescribable sweetness of delight along the way of the commandments of God; so that never departing from his authority and persevering in his teaching in the monastery until death, we may share in the sufferings of Christ by our patience so that we may deserve to be sharers with him in his kingdom' (Prologue 49–50).

If we are faithful to *lectio divina*, the time spent with scripture will be time for developing a personal relationship with God, and a relationship that will become central to our lives; indeed, it will help us find the path of life. And it will also help us grow and find fulfilment in a truly human sense.

This final chapter is less on how to do *lectio divina*, and more on what it does to us. One thing we should consider before we finish is to look at some of the hints the scriptures give about this process of growth and the goal towards which we are progressing. This can be considered as the development in us of the virtues that lie at the heart of Christian life, the virtues of faith, hope and charity. No less should it be seen in terms of the way we share by grace in the Trinitarian life itself; for we find our fulfilment in the divine life into which we are initiated by the sacramental life of the Church. This pattern of growth and fulfilment, however, needs to be understood in relation to the whole process of change that is taking place as God prepares us together with the whole of creation for its fulfilment in the new heaven and the new earth. These are very broad perspectives, but they are, I am sure, relevant to an understanding of life that is touched by the Resurrection of Jesus Christ, and our redemption by him.

When we engage deeply with the word of God, we are engaging with the word by which all things were made; the word of creation is the word of love that uttered us into existence. The word of creation is also the word of re-creation, the word of salvation, making all things new, the word that truly expresses the glory of God in the Kingdom for which we yearn and strive to prepare.

So if we live by the word in the way that *lectio divina* inculcates, the path of discipleship we follow will also be a path for the Lord to reach out through us to the world. The Spirit, whose presence we have discerned and to whom we seek to respond in our own lives, will be able to continue the work of redemption through us and bring the new creation to birth. When we say that the word is alive and active, as we must believe if we pray the scriptures in *lectio divina*, we do not just mean that the power of the word is confined to our hearts. Nothing can constrain the power of the Spirit. Our obedience to the word, however, opens up our lives as a channel for the Spirit, helps us act as instruments of divine grace so that God may bring his loving purpose to fulfilment.

Change in us makes for change in the world. The scriptures contain many passages that look forwards and help shape our imaginations with hope. In the same way the magnificent passages of apocalyptic in the Old and New Testaments, mysterious as they are, and they need rather more study for us to engage with them properly, can help us anticipate in our day the ways in which God is seeking to bring his new creation into existence.

That is the big picture forming the background to the main part of this chapter, in relation to which we may understand the process of growth and fulfilment in ourselves. This process comprises two sides. One side is the human side, a process of growth to human maturity. There are a number of passages in the letters of Paul, James and Peter that describe the process of development of a fully Christian character. The other side, seen, as it were, from God's point of view, is a process whereby we grow by grace into an ever deeper participation in the life of the Trinity. This theme is particularly important in the Gospel of John.

Daily contact with the word of God and engagement with the Holy Spirit brings us, by grace, into the dynamic of the life of the Trinity and our growth to Christian maturity as a growth to our full stature in Christ. This is an extraordinary fact, and too little understood. But *lectio divina* helps us perhaps more than anything else to learn how we are caught up by faith in the divine life itself. The Son is the Word of the Father, uttered by the Father; the Son's existence is love answering to the love with which the Father begets the Son. The Father speaks his word with the breath of the Spirit, which itself dwells in the Son, and which is for him too the breath of life. And this gift of the Spirit is totally free, poured out in love on all that God has made. It cannot be contained in itself. In *lectio divina* we listen to the Word by tuning in to the Holy Spirit that inspires the scriptures; the same Spirit dwells in our hearts by faith and enables our spirit to respond in faith, hope and love to the word of salvation we hear. The Word addressed to us becomes the Word in our own hearts, and unites us to the Lord who is our life. In our communion with the Word of God, by the power of the Spirit we come to share in the Sonship of Jesus himself, and are able to call God our Father as he did. Of course the process is analogous to the grace of the sacraments; but in the Christian understanding of things, word and sacrament go hand in hand.

A New Heaven and a New Earth

We read the scriptures, therefore, to help us understand what God is doing as he brings this new creation into existence. We read them in order to rediscover ourselves within this immense process of transformation; we may even begin to understand the part we are called on to play within it.

Jesus talks about new life. We can only understand what Jesus means in relation to what he says about the Kingdom of God; the new creation he promises will come into existence out of God's judgement on the present world we take for granted. But the Kingdom Jesus speaks of Jesus actually makes present now; though hidden as yet, it is already growing. It is something to be discovered through knowledge of Jesus. In several parables we get an impression of this.

Mark 4.26–29, 30–32

[26]And he said, 'The kingdom of God is as if someone should scatter seed upon the ground, [27]and should sleep and rise night and day, and the seed should sprout and grow, he knows not how. [28]The earth produces of itself, first the blade, then the ear, then the full grain in the ear. [29]But when the grain is ripe, at once he puts in the sickle, because the harvest has come.'

[30]And he said, 'With what can we compare the kingdom of God, or what parable shall we use for it? [31]It is like a grain of mustard seed, which, when sown upon the ground, is the smallest of all the seeds on earth; [32]yet when it is sown it grows up and becomes the greatest of all shrubs, and puts forth large branches, so that the birds of the air can make nests in its shade.'

These two parables remind us of the big picture within which we read and feed on the scriptures. The process of change *lectio divina* enables is also a gradual one, a process of change that easily escapes our notice. But where the Spirit is at work, there is life, and life is always directed to growth. We do not know how, but we can believe and hope in the unfailing power at work in our hearts.

Where *lectio divina* is giving shape to our lives, we can be sure that the Spirit is working in and through us to change the world. We may be daunted by our own insignificance, but everything depends, not on the physical scale of the seed, but on the life-giving power at work in it. We must not underestimate what God is able to do through us.

Sorrow Turned to Joy

This insight into the hidden reality of the Kingdom means that Jesus is able to talk about the sufferings of those who follow him in a positive way. They are inevitable, as some people hate the truth and persecute those who seek to live by it. But our sufferings are not sheer loss. In the Synoptic Gospels just before the story of his Passion, Jesus is recorded as talking about the end of the world; a time of suffering is inevitable, but it is within God's plan for the end time, the way he passes judgement on the world in order to redeem those who are faithful. In Luke's version, the note of confidence is strongest: 'Now when these things begin to take place, look up and raise your heads, because your redemption is drawing near' (Luke 21.28). 'By your endurance you will gain your lives' (Luke 21.19). John's Gospel avoids the vivid details of this narrative, which need to be understood in the context of Jewish apocalyptic writing. Instead, he uses an image of childbirth: 'Truly, truly, I say to you, you will weep and lament, but the world will rejoice; you will be sorrowful, but your sorrow will turn to joy. When a woman is in travail, she has sorrow, because her hour has come; but when she is delivered of the child, she no longer remembers the anguish, for joy that a child is born into the world' (John 16.20–21).

These are hopeful perspectives for us who often find our faith and hope under trial. St Paul speaks in the same way, but uses the image of childbirth more profoundly to describe the new creation itself.

Romans 8.18–25

[18]I consider that the sufferings of this present time are not worth comparing with the glory that is to be revealed to us. [19]For the creation waits with eager longing for the revealing of the sons of God; [20]for the creation was subjected to futility, not of its own will but by the will of him who subjected it in hope; [21]because the creation itself will be set free from its bondage to decay and obtain the glorious liberty of the children of God. [22]We know that the whole creation has been groaning in travail together until now; [23]and not only the creation, but we ourselves, who have the first fruits of the Spirit, groan inwardly as we wait for adoption as sons, the redemption of our bodies. [24]For in this hope we were saved. Now hope that is seen is not hope. For who hopes for what

he sees? [25]But if we hope for what we do not see, we wait for it with patience.

It is important for us to acknowledge our sense of suffering, our disappointments and frustrations; we need to learn that they are not inconsistent with the eagerness of our longing for God and his promise, rather they are just the inevitable shadow of our longing. Paradoxically, Paul sees that even our discontents have a part to play in the process of transformation. *Lectio divina* can teach us how to let all this be turned to longing and hope.

Our anxiety, too, about the future of our world, as well as for ourselves and those we love, is something we should also let come to the surface in our *lectio divina*. Anxiety is a sign of love and concern, beautiful sources of energy that also need to be redeemed and transformed, refocused on the world God is bringing into existence through our lives.

Growth of Christian Character

The sufferings of the present age are not only something patiently to endure; they are a positive influence on our personal growth.

Romans 5.1–5

[1]Therefore, since we are justified by faith, we have peace with God through our Lord Jesus Christ. [2]Through him we have obtained access to this grace in which we stand, and we rejoice in our hope of sharing the glory of God. [3]More than that, we rejoice in our sufferings, knowing that suffering produces endurance, [4]and endurance produces character, and character produces hope, [5]and hope does not disappoint us, because God's love has been poured into our hearts through the Holy Spirit which has been given to us.

Paul has much more in mind than a school of 'muscular Christianity'! The challenges we face in this world do more than toughen us up. He invites us to discover hope, and a God-given sense of hope, a source of strength because it draws its strength from knowledge of God's love, from a knowledge that the Holy Spirit is at work in us. Above all Paul invites us to discover peace, the gift of the Holy Spirit that crowns all his gifts.

That is to say, Paul believes that, whatever kind of suffering we have to endure, suffering is our way into the Paschal dynamic by which God brings new life out of death. This dynamic is central to the mystery of our faith, and it is a great thing to be able to reflect on this prayerfully in *lectio divina*. It is the way we can begin to learn that 'it is not I who live, but Christ lives in me' (Galatians 2.20).

Partakers of the Divine Nature

As a conclusion to the preceding section we would do well to take some time with the following excerpt, which links the formation of our human character with the life of grace that makes us sharers of the divine life.

2 Peter 1.3–8

[3]His divine power has granted to us all things that pertain to life and godliness, through the knowledge of him who called us to his own glory and excellence, [4]by which he has granted to us his precious and very great promises, that through these you may escape from the corruption that is in the world because of passion, and become partakers of the divine nature. [5]For this very reason make every effort to supplement your faith with virtue, and virtue with knowledge, [6]and knowledge with self-control, and self-control with steadfastness, and steadfastness with godliness, [7]and godliness with mutual affection, and mutual affection with love. [8]For if these things are yours and abound, they keep you from being ineffective or unfruitful in the knowledge of our Lord Jesus Christ.

Born Anew from the Word of God

New life entails a rebirth. Jesus is clear that new wine cannot be put into old wineskins (Mark 2.21–22). In his conversation with Nicodemus Jesus says we need to be reborn from above by the Holy Spirit (John 3.5), and several places in the New Testament speak of being reborn through the word of God. Some of these have already been given in the Introduction of this book.

1 Peter 1.22–25

[22]Having purified your souls by your obedience to the truth for a sincere love of each other, love one another earnestly from the heart. [23]You have been born anew, not of perishable seed but of imperishable, through the living and abiding word of God; [24]for 'All flesh is like grass and all its glory like the flower of grass. The grass withers, and the flower falls, [25]but the word of the Lord abides for ever.' That word is the good news which was preached to you.

We have already seen how the scriptures form a new community around Jesus. Listening to them, and hearing his voice in them, is not only learning what we have to do. In the first place, it is a remaking of our hearts, a new birth. Peter talks here of puri-fication and a growth in love. *Lectio divina* is a slow process, taking a lot of time, like conception and birth, for the new life of Christ to be formed in our hearts and minds.

James 1.16–18

[16]Do not be deceived, my beloved brothers and sisters. [17]Every good endowment and every perfect gift is from above, coming down from the Father of lights with whom there is no variation or shadow due to change. [18]Of his own will he brought us forth

147

by the word of truth that we should be a kind of first fruits of his creatures.

Lectio divina **helps us get our lives into perspective. The perspectives that ultimately matter are to see ourselves in relationship with God as our Father, and as responsible for the whole of creation. James here seems to have Psalm 8 in mind, and Adam as the head of creation, himself brought to life by God.**

If we are to see ourselves in the same kind of way, we need to learn to treasure our giftedness, to see it as God's gift to us, a refraction of his own perfection. Perhaps the hardest thing we have to learn is to be thankful for life as a gift; and we discover the meaning of life in learning to make it a gift to others. Such a new way of looking at things is the work of the Spirit in our hearts.

Measure of Stature of the Fullness of Christ

The New Testament talk about a rebirth is specifically a rebirth into Christ. The new life we live is Christ's, we in him and he in us. The life of faith is not only about human maturity. It is a process by which we grow more and more in the image of Christ, who lives human life to the full.

Ephesians 4.13–16

(God's gifts are for building up the body of Christ)[13] until we all attain to the unity of the faith and of the knowledge of the Son of God, to mature humanity, to the measure of the stature of the fullness of Christ;[14] so that we may no longer be children. ...
[15]Rather speaking the truth in love, we are to grow up in every way into him who is the head, into Christ,[16] from whom the

whole body, joined and knit together by every joint with which it is supplied, when each part is working properly, makes bodily growth and upbuilds itself in love.

This is the life we are trying to enter into by *lectio divina*; more than just trying to understand what is going on in the realm of grace, we seek to listen to Christ, to take his word into our lives and think and act like him. *Lectio divina* helps us to grow strong with his life. Faith respects our freedom; that is why this life is based on our understanding and loving acceptance of the word God addresses to us as free human beings. When we accept his word as the food of our life, the divine power of that word can work in our minds and hearts to make us share the life of the word we hear.

Rooted and Grounded in Him

The image in the following passage may recall Jesus' use of the tree as an image of faith. It starts as small as a mustard seed, but it grows to become the largest of trees, so that birds come and shelter in its branches. Another image was the vine (John 15). Jesus is the vine, we are the branches, and the Spirit is the sap that flows along them, uniting us in Christ and making our lives fruitful. Our human growth is shaped not only by the word of God, but also by the Holy Spirit. The Spirit that gives life is the Spirit that charges God's word with life for us.

Ephesians 3.14–19

[14]For this reason I bow my knees before the Father, [15]from whom every family in heaven and on earth is named, [16]that according to the riches of his glory he may grant you to be strengthened with might through his Spirit in your inner being, [17]and that Christ may dwell in your hearts through faith; that you, being rooted and grounded in

love, [18]may have power to comprehend with all the saints what is the breadth and length and height and depth, [19]and to know the love of Christ which surpasses knowledge, that you may be filled with all the fullness of God.

There are several passages in Paul that develop this line of thinking. We can compare, among others, Colossians 1.9–12. He regularly talks about knowledge, insight and other intellectual concepts as a sign of our growth in faith. He does not mean that being a Christian is about knowing lots, or being a clever person. He means that we need to be wise, to have sense of the things of God. Such wisdom is never an abstract thing; it is the ability to see things from God's point of view; above all, to have the kind of prophetic understanding that 'sees into' our situation and can discern the hand of God. Perhaps it will see his hand bringing the new creation to birth, or raised in judgement, or stretched out to heal and guide. In any case it will involve being able to pay attention to things and people, especially people, who are otherwise in danger of being forgotten. And always it will be to see with love.

This kind of wisdom is the fruit of *lectio divina*, for that is the way we learn to understand the ways of God and to see our world within the story of salvation.

Beholding the Glory of the Lord

In the second letter to the Corinthians Paul highlights how the Spirit is the source of a full understanding of scripture. Paul is comparing a Christian reading of God's word with that of the people of the Old Covenant. When Moses came down from Sinai having spoken with God face to face, the Israelites could not look at his face; he had to veil it. In the same way, they read the scriptures, as it were with their meaning veiled. For they did not understand them in the light of faith, the light of

Jesus Christ. The full meaning the Spirit is able to communicate to those who turn to him.

2 Corinthians 3.12–18

[12]Since we have such a hope, we are very bold, [13]not like Moses, who put a veil over his face so that the Israelites might not see the end of the fading splendour. [14]But their minds were hardened; for to this day, when they read the old covenant, that same veil remains unlifted, because only through Christ is it taken away. [15]Yes, to this day whenever Moses is read a veil lies over their minds; [16]but when someone turns to the Lord the veil is removed. [17]Now the Lord is the Spirit, and where the Spirit of the Lord is, there is freedom. [18]And we all, with unveiled face, beholding the glory of the Lord, are being changed into his likeness from one degree of glory to another; for this comes from the Lord who is the Spirit.

This remarkable passage teaches us how understanding the scriptures in faith as God's word to us sets us free. It makes us sons and daughters in the Son of God, the word that shapes our understanding. Rather surprisingly, the veil is described not as lying over the scriptures, as the analogy might suggest; it lies over our minds. For we all read the same text; the difference lies in us, in the resources available to our understanding. Faith means that the Spirit in our minds is able to help us interpret the true meaning of what we read. The Spirit then is at work in us as the source of our freedom, because he becomes the principle of our own lives.

The final verse develops the analogy of Moses. Unlike him we do not have veiled faces; *lectio divina* is our conversation with God face to face, but because we read in faith, our faces can shine out with the light of God's glory. We should reflect the truth of scripture in our lives. Developing the idea of human nature being shaped in the image of God, whom we can only see as if

reflected in a mirror, Paul thinks of us growing into a closer and closer likeness to God, and reflecting the glory of God as light by which others may see him.

Treasure in Earthen Vessels

It sounds too good to be true! Paul is well aware that we remain ordinary, weak and fallible mortals. But even that helps. We can never forget that we depend on God, and no one else should be under any illusions either. It is all grace. Not much further on in the same letter, Paul continues:

2 Corinthians 4.7–12

But we have this treasure in earthen vessels, to show that the transcendent power belongs to God and not to us. [8]We are afflicted in every way, but not crushed; perplexed, but not driven to despair; [9]persecuted, but not forsaken; struck down, but not destroyed; [10]always carrying in the body the death of Jesus, so that the life of Jesus may also be manifested in our bodies. [11]For while we live we are always being given up to death for Jesus' sake, so that the life of Jesus may be manifested in our mortal flesh. [12]So death is at work in us, but life in you.

Growth in the wisdom of the Spirit will never allow us to feel inflated; it is measured rather by our humility. For it is our honesty with ourselves that opens our hearts to receive what only God can give us; and it is always a gift, never something we can earn or deserve.

This passage also reminds us that our growth to Christian maturity in the spirit will be like Jesus', a growth by the way of the cross. In the spiritual dimension, growth is a matter of birth, death and rebirth, growth through transformation, not just development and extension.

Abiding in Jesus' Love

So far the passages we have been considering help us to think about how *lectio divina* transforms us, and helps us to grow into Christ. In John's Gospel this is explored in a different way. In this most intimate of Gospels Jesus is presented as dwelling in us by his word, so long as we dwell in him, and live by the word he speaks. In chapter 8 of that Gospel, several ideas from earlier on are brought together. The excerpts that follow omit the detail of the argument, which is worth reading in full.

John 8.31–32, 37b–38, 42–43

[31]Jesus then said to the Jews who had believed in him, 'If you continue in my word, you are truly my disciples, [32]and you will know the truth, and the truth will make you free.' . . .

[37b]'You seek to kill me, because my word finds no place in you. [38]I speak of what I have seen with my Father, and you do what you have heard from your father.' . . .

[42]Jesus said to them, 'If God were your Father, you would love me, for I proceeded and came forth from God; I came not of my own accord, but he sent me. [43]Why do you not understand what I say? It is because you cannot bear to hear my word.'

As he has said earlier on, belief in Jesus is based on hearing the word he has to speak, meaning recognizing it as a word from the Father. This is to understand what he has to say. Here Jesus adds the poignant remark that we fail to understand because we do not want to; we cannot bear it! We are stubborn and hard-hearted. Sometimes we find that the word of the scriptures touches our human indifference and neglect; it can confront us with our failings and sin. But there are times when it faces a harder audience and seems to make no difference. Here we see the mystery of divine grace, and need to recognize the

importance of prayer, that God will open the ears of people's hearts. Indeed there can be days like that for anyone. We need to make that prayer for our own sakes too.

But to listen and to hear, to understand, as Jesus calls it here, is to let his words find their place in us. They can be at home in us. It is a two-way process. Jesus begins by talking about our continuing in his word; the Greek verb for 'continue' also means to abide or dwell. His word is a place where we should make our home. This two-way process is very much what we try to do in *lectio divina*. The idea will be developed later on, when Jesus says that if we keep his word, he will dwell in us with his Father and the Spirit (14.23). The Word not only gives us a new birth, putting us in relationship to the Father; it is a source of communion with the Father in the Holy Spirit.

This is touched on in the passage here, when Jesus talks about the truth making us free. For the Holy Spirit leads those who hear Jesus' word into all truth (16.13).

It is worth trying briefly to examine how John develops this idea of the word of God as central to our relationship to God. The word of God is not just something said, but Jesus himself. It is how St John introduces us to Christ at the very start of his Gospel. To paraphrase, he says that from before all time, the Word exists in relation to God and is himself God; he is the source of creation, of life and light (John 1.1–3). This Word was made flesh and dwelt among us, living a human life (John 1.14). To those who received him, he gave power to become children of God (v. 12) through knowledge of the Father (v. 18). Receiving the Word, in this sense, introduces those who believe in Jesus to the same kind of relationship to the Father that the Word enjoys from before all time. We are 'in the word'. The words that Jesus speaks to us are therefore in a crucial sense a source of new life.

In the context of his conversation with Nicodemus in chapter 3, Jesus speaks about being born again, or being born from above (John 3.3–4).

Here the rebirth is through the Holy Spirit (v. 6), but again it depends on receiving the words that Jesus speaks (v. 11). The implication is that in receiving the words of Jesus, the Holy Spirit gives us a new birth into relationship with the Father. For in receiving in faith the word Jesus speaks we are reborn in the Word. The earlier chapters of this book have really only been trying to unpack how this can be understood. Here Jesus calls this entering the Kingdom of God.

In chapter 5, John returns to this theme. Here the context is more polemical: after the cure of the paralysed man, Jesus is arguing with Jews who refuse to believe. At the centre of the dispute is the place of scripture. You can read the scriptures, which bear witness to Jesus, and still fail to come to him in faith (5.39), or you can listen to his words and believe (5.24). To search the scriptures and to hear Jesus is to pass from death to life.

John 5.24, 37–40

[24]'Truly, truly, I say to you, everyone who hears my word and believes him who sent me, has eternal life; he does not come into judgment, but has passed from death to life. . . .

[37]'And the Father who sent me has himself borne witness to me. His voice you have never heard, his form you have never seen; [38]and you do not have his word abiding in you, for you do not believe him whom he has sent. [39]You search the scriptures, because you think that in them you have eternal life; and it is they that bear witness to me; [40]yet you refuse to come to me that you may have life.'

But the Jews Jesus is arguing with cannot do this because they do not have God's word dwelling in them. As the dispute sharpens in chapter 6, after the miracle of the loaves and Jesus' discourse on the Bread of Life, when many Jews began to drift away from Jesus, Peter sums up the position of those who continued to believe: 'Jesus said to the Twelve, ''Will you also go away?'' Simon Peter answered him, ''Lord, to whom shall we go? You have the words of eternal life; and we

know and have come to believe that you are the Holy One of God" '
(6.67–68).

This is directly relevant to understanding the power of *lectio divina*. For in this reading of scripture, we do pore over the text of the Jewish as well as the Christian scriptures and seek to come to Jesus; we do so because we can hear Jesus talking to us in them. The Word of God enables us to hear Jesus speaking in the words of scripture. We can hear them as the word of eternal life. In believing this word, we put our faith in Christ and pass into this new way of life centred on the Word, which is with the Father from the beginning. *Lectio divina* seeks to make our own the Word that gives Christian life its distinctive shape.

This is part of what Jesus says about the Holy Spirit in his last discourses with the disciples in John's Gospel:

John 14.15–17, 23–26

[15]'If you love me, you will keep my commandments. [16] And I will pray the Father, and he will give you another Counsellor, to be with you for ever, [17] even the Spirit of truth, whom the world cannot receive, because it neither sees him nor knows him; you know him, for he dwells with you, and will be in you. . . .'

[23]Jesus answered him, 'Those who love me will keep my word, and my Father will love them, and we will come to them and make our home with them. [24]Those who do not love me do not keep my words; and the word which you hear is not mine but the Father's who sent me. [25]These things I have spoken to you, while I am still with you. [26]But the Counsellor, the Holy Spirit, whom the Father will send in my name, he will teach you all things, and bring to your remembrance all that I have said to you.'

Hearing Jesus is not just listening to a story; it is about doing what he says, keeping his commandments. Jesus says a living faith like that is alive with the Spirit, which helps us grow in

knowledge and understanding, to live more fully, or 'abundantly' (compare John 10.10). It is interesting to note exactly what Jesus says: the Spirit leads us into all truth by reminding us what Jesus has himself said. Even though he has only spoken in what he calls veiled language (16.25), it is by dwelling on that, by remembering it and reflecting on it – what we have called 'meditating' on it – that we will grow in understanding.

So not only does the Word dwell in us with his Father (14.23) but the Holy Spirit is also at work in our minds and hearts. We are living the life of the Trinity, or it is living in us, because we have made the word our home. It is this Spirit-charged dynamic of life that Jesus calls his gift of peace.

John 15.7–14

[7]'If you abide in me, and my words abide in you, ask whatever you will, and it shall be done for you. [8] By this my Father is glorified, that you bear much fruit, and so prove to be my disciples. [9] As the Father has loved me, so have I loved you; abide in my love. [10] If you keep my commandments, you will abide in my love, just as I have kept the Father's commandments and abide in his love. [11] These things I have spoken to you, that my joy may be in you, and that your joy may be full.

[12]This is my commandment, that you love one another as I have loved you. [13] Greater love has no one than this, to lay down their life for their friends. [14] You are my friends if you do what I command you.'

In John's mind, this peace, this indwelling of the Trinity in Jesus' disciples, is a profound experience. It is a personal experience of Jesus himself, of his love and joy (vv.9, 11); but if it is an experience of his love, it should lead us to imitate his love, in laying down our lives for his friends (v.13).

Jesus' word also gives authority to our prayer (v. 7): the Father will give us whatever we ask because we have learnt to ask according to the will of the Father. But it is not just a private 'deal' with God. The Father is glorified in us, and we are proved to be Jesus' disciples and give glory to him, because we are obedient to the Father as Jesus was. This is the fruit we bring forth in abundance.

We ought to relate the line of thought implicit here to what Jesus had said earlier about his own word. He claims authority because he not only speaks, but also does what the Father commands him (4.34), and his message is true because he has seen the Father (3.32; 5.19–20). So for us who receive his word, and live by it to the end, Jesus can begin to talk plainly of the Father without using figures of speech, and we will really be able to pray in Jesus' name as yet we cannot (John 16.25–28; cf. 16–24).

Keeping Jesus' word changes us in our hearts, and also transforms our lives. It teaches us to live sacrificially, like Christ.

This is what Jesus has in mind when, after the discourse with his disciples, he prays to his Father for his disciples, for all who have heard him and, through them, will hear his word:

John 17.13–14, 17–19, 26

[13]'But now I am coming to you; and these things I speak in the world, that they may have my joy fulfilled in themselves. [14] I have given them your word; and the world has hated them because they are not of the world, even as I am not of the world. . . .'

[17]'Sanctify them in the truth; your word is truth. [18] As you sent me into the world, so I have sent them into the world. [19] And for their sake I consecrate myself, that they also may be consecrated in truth. . . .'

[26]'I made known to them your name, and I will make it known, that the love with which you have loved me may be in them, and I in them.'

Again the ideas are there of finding an experience of joy in keeping Jesus' word, and of knowing the truth. Here the truth is described as a source of holiness, a way whereby we share in Jesus' holiness. He consecrates himself for us; we find consecration in his word. By consecration, Jesus refers to his own death for our salvation. The holiness we are invited to discover is no less costly. At the end of the prayer, Jesus contrasts knowledge with ignorance of God; knowing Jesus is knowing the Father. But Jesus was killed because of that ignorance; making the Father's love known is not always welcome. But the love Jesus shares with us, the love he shares with the Father from all time, is a love we are called on to share with the world, in order to make his name known. And that is how we will know the love with which Jesus loves us and share his joy.

These are Jesus' last words before his Passion. It is a wonderful thing to listen to Jesus' own prayer of consecration to his Father, spoken in the midst of his disciples. It is beautiful to find ourselves, as we listen to these words, in the company of the Twelve, gathered around the table of the Last Supper, the supper that has become our feast of unity with the Lord, and in which we discover our communion with each other – albeit a communion that we know is fractured by our betrayals and lack of faith. But in the midst of our own weakness, we treasure the Lord's words that bear witness to his undying love. Every time we take the scriptures to ourselves, and seek to receive the word that the Lord addresses to each of us, we are invited to feast on his love, and find in him compassion, strength, wisdom and life.

A Final Word

And so we have come to the end of this book. To end, I would only like
to give a word of encouragement from my own experience of *lectio
divina*. I owe my discovery of *lectio divina* to a fellow student at university. I had read the Bible since I was a youngster, and at that level I
knew the stories quite well. Unsurprisingly for a regular churchgoer,
I was interested in the basis of Christian faith, and in the arrogance of my
teenage years, explored the 'discoveries' of biblical scholarship as well as
the vicissitudes of doctrinal history, exhilarated by the sense that authority over Christian faith could be subjected to criticism and so readily
'seen through'. All the time I was, unknown to myself, of course, under-
mining the grounds of my own faith, which, once I was at university,
began to founder and give way. Prayer was real, luckily. But when I
really needed God – and I knew in my bones God was the most real
thing there was – I could only hear an immense, rather chilly silence.

Two things saved me. First, I realized the fundamental importance of
the Christian community as the place where faith is owned and celebrated; it was a community's witness rather than a personal possession
you either had or had not. The Bible, which stands at the heart of all
Christian worship, was something to be listened to from within the faith
of the Christian community. It was a testimony to the origins and initial
growth of the faith of that community and its emergence from the long
religious development of God's people of the First Covenant. For that
reason, it was the judge and instigator of Christian life. Whatever should
be said about it by way of scholarly comment, its authority was not
because of its human authorship, nor was it understood when analysed
only in those terms. It was possible to conceive that the word of God

could be spoken in human language only by accepting that God has to use the limitations of human imaginations and the contingencies of human history to do so. God writes straight with crooked lines.

Second, I realized that God did speak, but I had never really listened to him. I had always done all the talking. The chilly silence haunted me, and once I got used to it a bit, it continually pulled me back towards it. It became a space where I began to make out the echo of the voice of what I had heard in the Bible. Or rather it helped me to listen to the silence and let the silence 'speak'.

There is a lot more that could be said, but it would stray beyond the purpose of this book. The point is that *lectio divina* is a way of learning to pay attention to God, and to listen to the word he speaks to each of us, wherever we are, whatever we are up to, with whatever questions and issues we are concerned. In spite of the length of this book, it is not difficult to learn. We can start, however weak or strong our faith. It is only a question of listening. It is more difficult to put into practice! But the difficulty there is the challenge of faith. And God has promised never to leave us in the lurch, if only we ask him for help and use the help he gives.

In the Gospel of John, Jesus likens himself to a good shepherd (John 10.1–18). He knows his own and his own know him. He calls each of us by name, and he leads us in and out. The sheep follow him because they hear his voice, and they know he is leading them out to good pasture as well as back into the safe keeping of his Father's sheepfold. I can hardly think of a more eloquent picture of what we can all discover in learning to listen and feed on the word of God we receive in the scriptures.

'I have come that they may have life and have life to the full.' If we want life and to see good days, God speaks to us, showing us the way to find it. We have only to follow his voice.